Why Do You Do This?

How To Recognize And Respond To Emotional
Blackmail, Verbal Abuse, And Codependent
Relationship Patterns

By Michelle Moore

Table of Contents

Introduction

My name is Michelle. I'm from New York City. An ordinary person living an extraordinary life. I'm a full-time traveler, working short-term online gigs, taking seasonal jobs in the countries where I happen to be. I've been doing this for more than a year now, I started in the middle of July, 2015. I'm about to quit and go home, wherever that may be.

This lifestyle is not as much of a fairy tale as it seems. I live paycheck to paycheck, sometimes I end up sleeping at the beach, but I have something more valuable than any money in the world. My peace of mind. Wonder why? Of course, there was a time when I didn't have peace, only chaos, fear, pain, anxiety, and self-hatred.

This trip was more like therapy and self-healing

to me. It wasn't easy to make the first step on this hundred-thousand-mile journey. But, I had to. I needed it. Without it, I would be in a nuthouse by now, or I would have committed suicide. So dark, and you're reading only the third paragraph. Don't worry, I see the sun is shining now, and brighter than ever. It wasn't always so.

I used to live in a very harmful, abusive, co-dependent relationship for more than three years. I went through all the possible layers of hell, I felt powerless, inferior and what's worse, totally useless. I loved him, hated him, would have loved to live without him, but couldn't. At least, that's what I thought. Until I met someone...

I'm a New Yorker – at least, I used to be until five years ago. Back then, I studied psychology at Columbia University. On top of that, I was an intern at *The Guardian,* and worked as a freelance web-designer for three startup companies. I was a busy girl with great prospects of living the American Dream. I felt strong, capable and full of potential. I thought nothing would keep me from achieving what I wanted. If you have stereotypes about New Yorkers, well, I pretty much fulfilled them all.

On a casual afternoon, after finishing my classes, I went to the Appletree Market on the corner of 120th and Amsterdam, and my whole life changed. The subject of the change was a six–foot-two, well-built, blonde, blue-eyed foreigner who spoke flawless English with a strong German accent. His smile was as charming as the kids smiling on the cover of an Osh Kosh B'gosh catalog. He looked like a modern Norse god.

He seemed slightly lost in the midst of Mamma Chia drinks, so I thought I would help him out. You know how lost extremely good-looking, obvious tourists can be. It turned out that one of his colleagues asked him to get some lemonade, but there was cranberry and strawberry flavored lemonade. The poor soul forgot which specific lemonade flavor he was supposed to get, so he stood there, hypnotized by the beverage shelf as if it would magically come up with the answer.

Knowing the gentleman's problem, and seeing someone so handsome so flummoxed, I found the situation extremely hilarious and adorable at the same time. With my quick wit, I suggested that he buy both of the flavors to reduce his chances of failure. I also added that the drink itself was tasty, so he could drink the one not chosen by his friend. Yes, I know, typical "I noticed you around, I find you really attractive, would you…um" movie-like situation. To give the moment a more romantic angle, he came up with a better deal. He suggested that he just dropped off the drink to the colleague and he'd give me the other one if I took the time to drink it with him.

Well, I took the time. At that moment I didn't know that in only four months I would leave everything behind to move to Mörfellden-Walldorf, a small town close to Frankfurt am Main in mid-west Germany. Does this seem a sudden twist in the story? It's no more sudden than it seemed to me to make this leap. It seemed that way to my strict, Harvard-bred father, who immediately excommunicated me from the family's heritage and our home for leaving Columbia for a "middle-class Norman, the German." Before you start wondering, I'm not Jewish.

Do you wonder how I could turn my back on my brilliant future and my seven-figure inheritance? Don't ask for a logical explanation, I don't have one, myself. I can only say that there and then it seemed like a good idea. It was the only feasible option I could conceive of in the most in-love period of my life.

However, this book isn't about me. I wrote a short introduction about myself to let you know that I wasn't always such a basket case. I had a good life with a promising career path, great university, wealthy family background, and many friends. I abandoned all of it for the promise of eternal love, children and tending sheep in a place like in *The Sound of Music*. It sounds cheesy, childish and incredibly stupid, but it happens to so many of us.

We all fall into that pit of a hazy daze and become reckless. When we are in love, the world stops around us. Except for two huge reflectors that illuminate our significant other and us, everything else in the world vanishes. There is nothing else on this Earth. Some get out of the daze with luck. When the pink clouds inevitably disappear, they still feel that they found their soul mate. They complement each other and develop a complex togetherness that consists of partnership, friendship, and a romantic relationship.

Others are not so lucky. Others meet someone, they think they have found the love of their life, but one casual Wednesday afternoon the cold shiver hits them that their relationship is not so magical as it seemed. They fight this feeling because it's a very painful realization. But, things won't get better. They'll start walking on eggshells to keep the relationship alive, which is simply not meant to be.

Here we arrive at the other person who changed my life. The fun factor is that I don't even know what her name is. I met her in a Starbucks on the Fourth of July, 2015, and spent only ten minutes with her. She was one of the most carefree, natural, generous, almost child-like and honest people I've ever met.

And she changed my life.

I count that day as not only the Independence Day of my nation but my own, too. Now, I know that changes are inevitable. They happen to all of us in each of our areas of life. However, change is bidirectional. There can be change for the better or for worse. If there is no improvement in something for a long time, only a madman invests all her energies into it. Emotional investment is one of the most demanding ones. If we invest a lot of positive energy in emotional life but receive either nothing or negative energy in exchange, that affects all the other areas, including friendships, career, free time and family.

This book is based on a true story. The story of a woman who loved, believed, was disappointed, fell deep down, got up, believed and loved. Her story is engaging, spirit-lifting, down-turning, enraging, heartbreaking but mostly instructive.

I wrote this book because I'm done. I'm healed. And I feel that with its help you can heal, too. I hope you'll use it wisely and extract what applies to you. Take the good, treat your wounds and leave out all the rest.

All relationships are unique, but good relationships are the same in one aspect: they grant you peace of mind — a mish-mash of trust, security and mildly constant happiness.

Chapter 1: Whoopi Goldberg?

I had a fight with Norman. It happened often, to my annoyance, but I couldn't help it. I felt it coming. We had a fight every three or four days. It lulled for the past six days. I *knew* it would come.

I sat in a Starbucks in Frankfurt on Kaiserstraße 20. I had been informed that my job application was rejected — again. I thought Frankfurt was the business capital of Europe! How could they reject me so many times just because I spoke horribly broken German? It was impossible to learn it!

I called Norman to tell him, hoping for a little compassion, but he was not receptive at all. Instead, he pointed out that I left home without feeding the dog, and I forgot he was expecting a package delivery and it was the least I could do for him since I didn't have an actual job and nothing else to do.

I tried to defend myself. The dog still had some food when I left. I tried to apologize for the forgotten package. I reminded him that I had asked him to reschedule the delivery because I went to Frankfurt to try to get a job. He ignored me, muttered something in German and hung up. I was totally heartbroken. I knew that this discussion was far from over and I would get my face-to-face dosage of anger later. I felt so helpless that I started to cry when someone called me by name.

"Hello, Michelle!" She was probably the same age as me but seemed much younger. She had smooth, gentle features, her eyes smiled wider than her lips. She was fit, tanned, and dressed like Jeanie from *Hair,* carrying a huge green backpack.

I thought, *Please don't ask for money*... I asked, "How do you know my name?" I was sullen, trying to dry my eyes from the tears.

She just pointed to my untouched caramel latte

cup. The barman had cheerfully asked my name and I had totally forgotten since I had bigger problems to think about. "Oh, okay," I nodded, and stared blankly in a different direction.

I hoped she'll clear off if I showed disinterest. Instead, she sat in the chair next to me. My old self would have opposed, but my truncated self-esteem didn't have the power or the courage to protest and make her leave. I took a quick glance at her, and when I realized she was looking at me intensely, I turned my gaze again. Somehow, I felt that she could see right through me. I felt she *knew*.

"You look terrible," she stated after a few seconds.

Yeah, I know, I thought, but I didn't say a word, I just stared into space.

"What's wrong?" she asked.

I hesitated for a moment, but I felt such a need to tell someone about my misery that I couldn't keep it in. I had cut relations with my parents, my American friendships faded with time, and locals didn't meddle too much with the *Ausländer*. This woman was here, spoke English and seemed interested. She spoke with an accent, she may have been Russian or some other Slavic country. I didn't care. I felt alone and needed attention and understanding.

"I just spoke with my fiancée, and I think I made him angry. I always do. I knew I shouldn't have said those things and that I could have handled things better. I know what he'll do when I get home. Ugh, I don't even want to go home... But if I don't, he might leave me. No wonder he's had enough. I know it doesn't make sense what I say, but..." My entire body trembled with repressed tears, my hands awkwardly grasped the now-cold caramel latte. I felt that excruciating dumpling in my stomach and stifling sensation around my throat that I always felt when the slightest thought of losing him crawled into my mind. I couldn't go on saying these thoughts out loud, it was too painful. I didn't want to think about losing him, I didn't want to feel this way. The only thing that could deter my bewildered thoughts were some other self-blaming that eased my worried mind.

"It makes perfect sense," she replied before I could have said another fearful sentence. "You feel as you're not enough, you mess up most of the time because you're inadequate and your fiancée is much better. You feel like you're lucky to have him, and nobody will ever love you as he does. And if you lose him, there is no place on Earth left for you."

For a moment I forgot about my sickening restlessness. *Who is this woman? How does she know exactly what I feel – and fear?*

"Am I right?" She gave me the look a teacher would give when they caught the student cheating on the test.

I nodded.

"If I'm right, that means that you also know, somewhere deep down, that all these negative beliefs about yourself are not true. You can't live like this! I bet you wish for peace of mind, but you never truly have it. As soon as a calmer period starts—and I'd like to emphasize that I didn't say happier on purpose—you start getting anxious about the next thing you'll mess up. You walk on eggshells, but soon something bad will happen again, and the whole fear circle restarts.

I was surprised, shocked, and interested all at the same time. I wanted to listen more to this woman. I wanted her to tell me more about my thoughts, I felt that she truly understood me and knew what I was going through after only a few minutes of acquaintance. She got up, grabbed my caramel latte, and took a huge sip of it. She was a cheeky one, I had to give her that. However, I didn't care that much about my drink. My stomach was the size of a peanut, I couldn't have drunk it anyway.

"I must go now, I have a plane to catch," she said casually. "But before that, allow me to give you something." She started looking for something in her oversized green backpack. Finally, she fished out what she was looking for and handed it to me. It was an old, beat up, thick, copybook with Winnie the Pooh on the cover. When she handed me the copybook she said something I shall never forget.

"My journal, my savior and yours, if you want it. This is not a love story. This is a story about the power of love and the influence it has over people. It's a collection of mistakes we make, signs we ignore, and unhealthy behavioral patterns we tend to repeat. And, of course, it has the antidotes that only someone who learned the hard way can share, repeatedly falling prey to her own lack of awareness. I hope it will help you see clearer and make your decision accordingly."

With that said, she cheerfully walked out of Starbucks with my caramel latte. If I haven't had her Winnie the Pooh journal in my hands, I probably would have thought that I hallucinated the entire encounter. I felt like I was in a movie where Whoopi Goldberg or Morgan Freeman appear as a deity and help the main character with something. But my deity was pretty, blonde and looked like a hippie surfer girl.

Chapter 2: Emotional Hunger

This is where the story begins. Not only mine, but hers and I feel I can be so bold to say, all of ours who ever experienced a toxic relationship. This is a story for, and about, all men and women who feel that something's terribly wrong in their relationship.

The relationship you're in doesn't have to be in as terminal a stage as mine was to need fixing. The mistakes and solutions the journal presents can help you figure out and solve small issues before they get nasty. It can also guide you through a breakup or ease post-breakup traumas.

I wish I could have asked her permission to publish her journal entries. For the sake of the characters' privacy I changed the names and locations in some of the entries. I don't know her name since she never introduced herself. On the cover, however, she carved two letters: E. D. She never mentioned her name in the journal, so I chose to name her based on my first instinct, that she is Russian, and gave her the name Elena. To stay true to the E.D. monogram I named the main character of her stories Dimitri.

Now let's go back to the Fourth of July, 2015. Elena left and I sat in Starbucks, still trying to understand what had just happened. I held her diary in my hands. I was tempted to start reading it, but my mind was troubled. I still wandered back to the disturbing conversation I had with Norman. Why couldn't he be more patient with me? Where was the sweet prince in a white Volkswagen I fell for? What would happen with my dreams? Then Elena's words echoed into my mind: "not good enough", "walking on eggshells", "there's something wrong", "peace of mind". Peace of mind...

I opened the diary. On the very first page I saw a quote. **"First love never ends but always comes to an ending."** Unknown author. Next to it there was a pink star-shaped post it with the following note: "I got this quote in a fortune cookie two days after our break-up. Things always happen for a reason."

Reading this made me feel very uncomfortable. I fought against the idea that the quote was true in my case, even if I was a woman of science. I knew psychology, I knew how the chemistry of the emotion we call love worked. Serotonin, dopamine, and norepinephrine invaded the brain and body. They gave intense energy, sweet sleeplessness, flushed skin, sweaty palms – all of that. However, after one, maybe two years they inevitably burn out. I knew all of it but I couldn't accept it to be true to me. I felt we were a different kind of couple, special, the exception, not the rule. I was very close to just leaving the journal there and to run home to go on with my misery. But something told me to keep reading...

October 1st, 2006.

I arrived yesterday to the new town 1500 miles from home. I've never been so far from home before, neither felt so alone and vulnerable.

Everything happened so fast. My grandparents dying, my mom falling ill, me getting fired... What a year...

My dad just left me here two hours ago, leaving with the train, going east. Going home. His eyes were full of tears as he waved goodbye. I didn't cry, I had to stay strong. I had to make a living here, in this town, not to stay an out-of-work burden on him. Who knows when will I see him again?

I feel alone. My heart aches with so much loss. And I'm afraid. I feel I have no future ahead of me....

It gets dark early here in the north. I don't like the dark. From now on I will live in a shared room, namely Room Number Six, in a governmental apartment. Fun fact, this building served as a train wagon factory and an army depot in World War II. I will have two roommates apparently. I hope they will be nice. Hopefully, they won't be creeps. Oh, how much I wish to rent my own apartment. Soon, soon I will.

October 2nd, 2006

The first night alone was horrible. The only entertainment I could find was the gatekeeper's book that he loaned me. It had the title *Cujo*, by Stephen King. It's about a huge, aggressive dog. To be honest, I don't even know what it's about. I never made through page twenty. When the dog appeared, right then a huge thunder broke the silence outside. Creepy northern weather. I locked the book outside the room. I didn't want to coexist with it in the same space for a minute more. I pledge here on this page that I shall never read Stephen King again.

October 6th, 2006

My two roommates are weird but kind. One is 230 pounds and a rocker girl who has a skinny boyfriend. She's madly in love with him and her favorite topic is how many orgasms she had during their weekend. She also snores like a cannon. I need to buy earplugs. My other roommate smokes weed, she's in a chaotic relationship and she's borderline suicidal when drugs, drinks, and disputes hit her at the same time. Last night I had to pull her back through the window, holding her waist. She wanted to die because she had a fight with her boyfriend. We live on the first floor so she probably wouldn't have died, but still, it's better to pull her back than to ice her leg all night. It happened with her last year according to my other roommate.

My notes:

Clearly, Elena had a different life than I did. Her early years must have been financially very challenging. It seems she came from a poor family and she was a go-getter. When I read these pages, my heart crumbled at her sad story, but I had to laugh at her journal descriptions. She had such a good, self-deprecating humor that made me feel less bad about her misery. It seemed she was a positive person who didn't take herself too seriously. Based on our ten-minute encounter I could confirm that.

There were other stories in her journal, but for the sake of the book's fluency I won't share all of them. Next to the entries there were colorful post-its, or large sheets of paper folded and attached. She did a thorough self-evaluation job on her early thoughts, apparently.

Elena's notes:

Indeed, I never read Stephen King ever since. Sorry, Master.

I traveled in ninety-eight countries in the past few years. I met many people during my travels. All I asked them about were relationship questions. I felt like I was on a mission – heal and seek healing. Each story touched me. Each story gave me perspective and important lessons.

I spoke with more than six hundred couples and singles all around the world, made notes about their problems, solutions, and well-working relationship routines. Those who lived in an unbalanced, bad, or toxic relationship had one thing in common: they craved love and belonging as their life depended on it.

How can hunger for love take such an extreme

form? Who are the most exposed to experience hunger for love? The answer: people who feel neglected, who changed their previous lifestyle completely, who live on their own from a young age, who have an ill parent, who grew up in a broken family, or live in a dysfunctional family. They are much more vulnerable and hungry for love than those who don't experience these hardships. Those who don't get enough love for one reason or another are willing to sacrifice or endure much more, to get even a fraction more of love. Loss and feeling helpless can easily make them targets of emotional, physical, or financial exploitation.

We all have to examine whether we've been severely affected by one or more hardships mentioned above before we engage in a relationship. If we are in a relationship, it is still good to do this examination. Many problems we might face can be tracked back to our, or our partner's, hunger for love rooting in a previous lacking.

I can see now that all I experienced, in those three years in my relationship with Dimitri, were the result of a desperate hunger for love. My life changed, my grandparents died, my mom got ill, I moved, I was alone. I didn't have anybody around to stand up for me when I was bullied, nobody to hug after a long day. No one else cared about my everyday problems. No wonder I traded in my right mind when I finally met someone to love. I clung onto him with ten nails like a cat in a mosquito net. I didn't want to leave the relationship even when it was much worse than being alone.

I see this now, and I don't regret it. All I want is to do things differently in my future relationship. I want to reap the fruits of the long lessons I've learned and be smarter the next time. I'm sure I'll face some hardship, but not same hardships, not the same problems. I will strive to correct my new mistakes and become a little bit better as a person every day. This is what life is about, after all, a never-ending trail of improving and learning.

When we want to improve something – it doesn't matter if it is our romantic life, work, attitude towards a belief or action, we have to start improving that part we have total control of: our own mind. Before engaging in a relationship, or improving the existing one, we have to make sure to treat our hunger for love, otherwise, it will make us vulnerable and over-consenting.

What is hunger for love?

Hunger for love is pure emotional hunger. As a matter of fact, it has nothing to do with love, but with the needs caused by deprivation earlier in life. It is a primitive condition of longing. People want to avoid the emptiness related to aloneness and separation. These needs can never be fully satisfied with a relationship. In fact, it is exploitive and destructive to the partner. Each party ends up exploited in this sort of codependent relationship: the one who has emotional hunger issues and is willing to sacrifice much more to get the love, and the other party whose conscious or subconscious purpose is to be a love giving machine. It's simply not fair.

I was very hungry emotionally, I tolerated emotional and physical abuse, but I wasn't innocent, and certainly not a victim. My partner never did anything to me that I didn't enable him to do, Or that I didn't choose to accept. Staying silent, threatening without being conscious of it, and unreasonable, hoping for things to change, is acceptance, and therefore an accomplice in the crime.

I feel like I'm making lots of notes on the subject of analyzing personal background, but I have to. This is the key momentum that defines the relationship to become a partnership or a (co)dependency."

"It is wise to be suspicious of your own use of the word 'love' or 'I love you.' If you search yourself truthfully you may discover that you say these words most often, not when you feel the most for others, but rather when you experience strong dependency needs and feel the need for reassurance."

Dr. Robert Firestone

There are always signs that indicate why we have emotional hunger. Things we feel, things that motivate us, things we do – or don't do. All these can be signs. For example, if we feel motivated to help somebody out just to get recognition in exchange, that's not right. That's a selfish act where we need something from them, and to get it we're okay with sacrificing our time and energy. However, doing this is exhausting and often backfires. (I'm not talking about business-related helping.)

Maybe you help people to get words of affirmation. You help them so you can ask for help at some point, but you feel that you would not be worthy enough to ask for help unless you made them 'indebted' before. Or, you help to be considered nice and generous, because you need people's recognition and acceptance. This behavior isn't pure altruism, but rather exploitation. You trade yourself in exchange to avoid the fear of being disliked and remaining alone.

During the honeymoon months of my relationship with Dimitri, I ended up demonizing solitude. I feared it so much that even when being alone was clearly the better option, I still considered being in a harmful, emotionally abusive relationship much safer and less frightening than alone. Why?

We often confuse solitude with loneliness. Both are a state of mind. Solitude is actually a necessary part of a self-aware, auto-critical and wise way of living. Socrates, the great Athenian philosopher's golden saying states that "The unexamined life is not worth living." Self-knowledge is the fundamental result of solitude. Auto-reflection will tell more about us than any book, teacher, or philosophy. It involves our individual intuition, not the intellect.

To practice solitude and introspection, we don't have to be single, just like being single doesn't mean we'll be lonely. Loneliness is an emotional response to lack of companionship. It can occur in the room where we sit with our partner just as easily and often as if we're by ourselves. The only achievement we can get by staying in an unhealthy relationship is that we avoid being alone. But, we'll still be lonely.

Many single people I met who experienced long-term, unhappy relationships claimed they felt much better and relieved after they finally made the big step of breaking up. They didn't feel lonelier than before, and what's more, many felt much less lonely after the breakup because they reconnected with friends and family — bonds they neglected during the relationship.

When we feel that we'd be better off without a relationship, but fear keeps us there, it's time to make peace with the thought of being alone in solitude without being lonely. How? I collected the best answers to this question.

> "I feared to leave a bad relationship because I felt that I invested too much time into it. When I realized that each minute, week or year invested was not wasted, but added to the person who I am now, and built my character in separate ways seemed less scary. I have also noticed that each minute, week or year spent in this relationship was a theft from the rest of my life. So *dodge the excuse of time*." (Marta, 34, Las Palmas)

> "We had an apartment together, some

investment properties and a cat. I was so terrified what would happen with them if I handed the divorce note in. I had little faith in my partner, and stubbornly decided that the woman takes it all, so I stayed in that unhappy marriage for years when finally my wife handed the divorce note in. She was fair, all things were divided without any problem. Now I feel regret that I didn't hire a lawyer to explain to me how divorce works out of pure laziness and comfort. The greatest lesson I've learned is to *never stay in a broken marriage for the stuff.*" (Gregory, 41, Birmingham)

"I hoped for so long. I hoped that he'd change, be kinder, go out more – he didn't. Now I realize that if someone doesn't take the trouble at the beginning of the relationship when you are in the campaign period, they're less likely to do it later. If somebody doesn't make you happy as he or she is, that's a big sign that you're not meant to be together. You'll just have expectations that your partner will never meet. And he will suffer because he'll feel that he's not good enough since he's not meeting your expectations. Both of you will suffer. A year after the breakup I met a wonderful man who completes my sentences. I'm so very happy now, and so is my ex." (Helga, 27, Hamburg)

"I'm sixty-six and I'm getting divorced. Isn't that crazy? My friends whisper behind my back that I'm an old fool, what do I expect to find at this age? They are right, I'm a fool. I'm a fool because I didn't take this step thirty years ago. I always feared that if I did it, I'd regret it. I thought regret was something you feel when you wake up alone in your bed, or when you go home to an empty house. But these are not feelings connected to regret, just bad feelings you experience in a transitional period. Then you get used to them and feel okay again. Regret, my dear, is the feeling that comes when you're sixty-six and realize that you've spent your life with the wrong person." (Samuel, 66, Chicago)

Some fear breaking up because they think that there's nobody else out there for them. They think themselves incapable of trapping another person. I'd like to point out the big stupidity-paradox of this belief, though I am sorry for the phrasing. I've been here too, so I can badmouth this attitude: you are in a relationship, you're right in one which you're about to leave. What greater proof do you need than this that you're able and capable of trapping someone? It happened once, so sure as Band-Aids in swimming pools that it will happen again.

Chapter 3: Judgment Free

November 18th, 2006

I didn't get the job. After my trial weeks ran out, they sent me away with minimum wage. I protested, but in vain. I think this is their business model. They hire people for a few weeks, then fire them and save a lot of money. I'm not even sure if it's legal. My savings are running out. I made a deal with the gatekeeper that he brings me food if I help with his crosswords competition with the other gatekeeper. My suicidal roommate wanted to jump again, and my other roommate had a total of eight orgasms this week. I'm really starting to feel like the only sane person here. Tomorrow I go to other job interviews.

November 23rd, 2006

I have a job! And it's a good one. I've gotten lucky. I hope I can move out from the nuthouse in a few months. I started calling our room "Ward no.6", after Chekhov's book. At my age I really shouldn't live in a shared room with other, younger girls. They are both in love in different ways. I'm the virgin who's never been in love before. I wonder what it feels like.

Elena's notes:

I feel that I was very judgmental back then when I wrote these journal entries. I had a very strict script on how things were supposed to be. "I'm not supposed to live with others at age X, I'm not supposed to be a virgin." I judged my roommates by living differently and so on. These judgments didn't make me smarter. In fact, they closed up all the possibilities of improvement.

[Off topic: I'd really recommend people who're interested in self-improvement to keep an honest journal about their thoughts where they write down some lines periodically. It's a great mirror, and also an improvement measurement tool. I'm so grateful that I wrote this journal.

Now that the time has come to take some serious contemplating about myself, I have a very accurate mirror in front of me.]

Right now I'm in Bali, it's 2014, sitting at a solitary café with a great view, contemplating why was I so stressed and judgmental, and why people were in general.

Non-smokers pointing fingers at smokers and vice versa. Top achievers in class labeling other students as "dumb," while slackers call the achievers "bookworms." Poor badmouthing the rich, and rich looking down on the poor. I could go on with the list, but what is common in these examples?

That *people judge based on their differences*. They are less likely to judge those who are more similar to them in habits, lifestyle or values. In psychology, this behavior pattern is called *equal status contact*. This seems obvious, but I bet we rarely think about why we judge others. We instinctively repel things and people who don't share our point of view.

Something we don't often do seems morally or

socially incorrect for us until we do it ourselves. For example, cheating seems unacceptable and outrageous, and we demonize cheaters. When we cheat on our partner for one reason or another, everything is shown in a different light. Or, to use the example of my roommate suffering from *histrionic personality disorder,* I considered her crazy and theatrical, I judged her. However, when I went through similar relationship problems as her, the reactions she gave didn't seem so unreasonable anymore.

The more you experience, the less judgmental you'll become. This is why I never believed the nonsense of learning from others' mistakes. You can't. You may get the theory of that lesson, you can make a mental note about being mindful about it, but you won't get the empirical knowledge. As you could see in the paragraph above, without personal experience, you can't understand others' motivations unconditionally.

This doesn't mean that you should go through all the nine circles of Dante's Inferno to understand everyone empirically. It's merely a fact that what you experienced on your own helps you relate more accurately to others without a negative bias.

To reduce the conflict and encourage communication between people with differing values, lifestyles or beliefs, first they should be brought to a level where they can be of equal status. In other words, we have to find a common ground. This is what equal status contact is about[1] – interaction on the same level. As soon as we're on the same level, it's less likely to be hostile based on differences. For example, if a communist and a capitalist start talking based on their political views, they may break into a personal cold war. However, if they are both basketball lovers, they like Kevin Durant, and they have a conversation about that first, they'll probably build mutual sympathy. This might be enough to handle their political viewpoints more smoothly and be less judgmental about it later. "He is a communist, but a very nice person," sort-of attitude.

---

[1]

http://www.alleydog.com/glossary/definiti on.php?term=Equal-Status+Contact

It can cause a lot of trouble in a relationship if people have fixed ideas about how things are supposed to be as I did. Even if you agree upon a lot of things, it's impossible to agree on everything. When you inevitably touch upon topics, which you don't agree on, fights will follow. Depending on the issue, they can become deal breakers. You shouldn't compromise your core values, but if you stick to your guns with something you didn't experience, just deciding that "this how it's supposed to be," you may be wrong and cause unnecessary pain for yourself.

The second thing, after healing the hunger for love, I figured one should change about themselves before engaging in a relationship: *inflexibility, and quickness of judgment.*

It's crucial to be flexible, accepting and open-minded toward our better half and partner in life, be it a short or long-term relationship. Differing on the question of having children, marriage or small town versus metropolis living are real deal breakers. Sport preferences, or dishwashing habits shouldn't be.

I met a man in New Zealand whose relationship ended because he consumed too much water when dishwashing. I'm not joking. It's nice to be environmentally conscious, but there are alternative solutions that are less harsh, like an economically-programmed dishwasher, or overtaking this chore activity. The poor man just wanted to help, and he didn't understand his girlfriend's problem. He labeled her as ungrateful. Neither of them communicated clearly about their problem and values.

They didn't find the good equal status contact: the girl was an environmentalist; the guy was trying to help her with chores. What could have been a good contact point for them was their shared value of being supportive. The woman supported the environment, the man supported the woman. Trying to talk to each other through that contact point would have made it easier for them to understand how the other felt. "Oh, honey, to me, helping the environment feels like helping me feels to you. I appreciate it. But please, let's find a solution where both of our helping preferences can thrive."

If you can't get your message through to your partner, try to phrase it in a way he or she can understand. A very simplistic example, if you have a broken arm, but your partner never did, he won't understand how painful and annoying it is. If you point out to him that it is as painful and annoying as it was for him to have a broken leg, a different, but similar situation, he'll understand it better, because you apply to something he experienced first hand.

Chapter 4: Love Has Many Faces

December 2nd, 2006

"I just discovered that there is a training center in the other part of the building, and a piano. I feel that everything about this place is a little bit grotesque. I started practicing piano there. Around six p.m. a few men showed up at the training center, and started practicing some martial arts. "

December 19th, 2006

"Today I just finished my piano lesson when the teacher, called "sensei", came to me to ask if I wanted to join their karate group. I told him that I don't have money. He said I could come for free for a while if I teach him piano in exchange. I said okay. I feel happy about this unexpected invitation. I still don't know many people here and really want to feel like I belong in a group."

December 27th, 2006

"I'm home. Finally, I'm home and I spent Christmas with my family. Better phrased, with my families. My mom's condition stabilized, but she is still very sick and mentally unstable. My dad, on the other hand, has a new family – a woman and her daughter. We spent Christmas Day with them, too. I understand that my father is a healthy man in his late forties. He needs a real woman beside him. Also, he claims that he is very much in love with her. I can see why. She is independent, and ten years younger. She also was diagnosed with cancer recently. I can see her side, too, wanting to be with a man like my dad. I want my father to be happy, so I have no objection and I really want to accept and grow to love them. But, it's so hard to lie to my mother every day. She seems oblivious to my dad's parallel life, so no damage is done, I guess."

Elena's notes:

Love can have many faces. Sometimes it is difficult to understand them. The triangle of my dad, mom, and dad's girlfriend was the same. If I looked at it plainly, I'd have said that my dad is a horrible person, cheating on my mom.

Since I tried to approach it through a contact point, which was the feeling of loneliness and the hope for belonging, I could understand him and all his actions seemed considerate and sensible. My mom was mentally ill, and technically not herself for years. My dad was a vivacious, healthy man, who chose to stay by my mother's side since she had no one left. He chose to do the right thing, but right things don't make us happy all the time. He found love and embraced it. Luckily his girlfriend accepted his situation. Everybody was happy. How twisted and perfect it was!

My dad's girlfriend sometimes sent food to my mom. She was a truly special person, the only healthy female authority figure I had. And, as it usually happens with good people, she died of cancer last year.

Being quick to judge and condemn what people do or how they live without seeing the full picture is a very harmful action. Yet, all of us do it. We can't completely get rid of being judgmental, but we can strive to be better, judge less, be more mindful and take the time to familiarize ourselves with a situation before we pose an unfair verdict and hurt someone.

Where better to start than our own surroundings? I used to be very quick to judge and executed harsh verdicts in my relationship. My dad's case was an exception where I chose to be understanding. But, considering my ex-boyfriend, I always assumed the worst when it came to an exchange of opinions.

I have to add that many times he was intentionally malicious, but I didn't help the situation with my constant doubts, defensive behavior, and quick judgment either. Even if he wanted to improve his behavior, I didn't let him. I didn't show him the trust I should have to make him feel that I believed in his improvement.

Oftentimes people live up to our expectations — if those expectations are low, then no wonder they'll act accordingly. Why should they try to be better if we already have decided to treat them in a certain dismissive way?

"Give people a good reputation they can live up to." This is what I read in *How to Win Friends and Influence People* by Dale Carnegie. And it works! I often use this technique with people nowadays, "someone as talented in writing as you are shouldn't do this", or "I know that you are an excellent driver", or "I trust you don't mean to harm me when you say this but please know that it hurts me." I consider these positive manipulations. When a request or a critique is packaged in positive words, people are more likely to listen. Their ego won't let them act otherwise.

The good reputation we tell to others must not be a lie. If it's a lie, then all we do is an ill-mannered manipulation. There must be some truth in what we tell people as a positive reputation to live up to.

People who instantly assume the worst usually had a bad experience in their previous relationships and radiate it to the current one.

"I used to be very quarrelsome with my Fabio. For some reason, I thought he would cheat on me each time he went out with his friends. I thought he went out with friends with the purpose to make me scared— it was so stupid of me. Luckily we could talk it through, he understood that I had been cheated before, that's where my fear comes from, so now he texts a bit more often, and sometimes takes me with him. I'm so glad that he is so understanding, and I could open up about my irrational judgment issues." (Carla, 29, Firenze)

Others lack confidence, and that's why they judge so quickly. They try to hide their own fear.

"My ex-girlfriend was very okay with herself, I don't even understand why she chose me as a partner. The short time we were together was very frustrating to me because I never felt good enough for her. I even thought she was confident just to make me feel even worse about myself. I started berating her – first subconsciously, then, I'm ashamed to confess, consciously. I told her judgmental things to cut her wings and drag her to my confidence level. I never congratulated her, was happy when she was successful, it made me feel good when she didn't feel good about herself. I feel so bad about it now. I'd like to improve, but she left me because she was self-aware enough to catch on to what I was doing. I feel so horrible..." (Louis, 32, Nice)

Confidence doesn't happen in an instant and doesn't cover all of our areas of life. Confidence comes from doing things repeatedly with success. The more the action is repeated successfully, the more secure people feel about it. The more difficult the action is, the more repetitions it will require to master it and build confidence around it.

For example, if someone cooks scrambled eggs

many times, after a few occasions he will feel confident about his scrambled eggs-making technique. This doesn't mean that he'll be instantly confident in cooking beef wellington. Mastering that menu requires more time and practice.

Also, if someone is confident in his cooking skill, that doesn't mean that he'll be equally confident in relationship communication. That's why I think confidence is a misunderstood and overrated concept. People think about it as some superpower that once achieved will make them invincible, but that's far from the truth.

Our excessive struggle to gain confidence can lead us to do unfair and unreasonable things, as Louis' case proves. He wanted to gain confidence by undermining his girlfriends'.

He didn't think his actions through. Taking away someone's confidence won't give him more. He also ignored the harmful effect of comparison. Comparison is never a good tool to gain confidence. It's deceitful. As long as we compare ourselves to someone less confident than us, we'll feel relieved and empowered. As soon as we meet someone with higher confidence, we'll crumble like a house of cards. Seeking people with the same level of confidence blocks the chance for improvement.

This is why we should never measure our own worth, confidence or any other trait to others, only ourselves. We shouldn't try to do anything else but become one percent better than we were the day before. That's the best thing we can do to stay balanced, decrease fear and judgment, and become more confident by practicing self-improvement each day.

Focus on yourself. Your actions, your attitude, your improvement. If Louis would have done that they might still be together. When in a relationship, the "you and me" becomes "us". However, inside the "us bubble" there is still a small you and me bubble. If you find a flaw in yourself, don't try to change it by changing your partner.

Courage can make the real difference. You don't have to be confident to be courageous. Building courage is like throwing yourself off a cliff and assembling the wings during the fall. Courage is admitting flaws, lack of confidence, sacrificing your truth for the sake of peace. Taking the first step is the real deal.

Repeated courageous actions will make you confident as a result.

Decrease your judgments, increase your courage, give people a good reputation to live up to and don't give confidence too much credit. Courageous actions saved more relationships than confident ones.

"Ego is how we want the world to see us.
Confidence is how we see ourselves."
Brian MacKenzie

Chapter 5: The Twisted Relationship of Abuse With Shame

December 30th, 2006

I had to go back to Ward No. 6. My roommates didn't work on New Year's Eve, but I chose to for the higher wages. I came back late. There were some construction workers temporarily situated on the second floor. I'm afraid of them. They are all men, they drink in the evening, and I'm the only woman here. I don't want to be judgmental, but I'm concerned."

January 1st, 2007

"I had the most frightening experience last night. I got back to my room relatively early on the 31st, and I saw the workers playing cards in the kitchen. They asked me to join them. I didn't want to spend my New Year's Eve alone, and I didn't dare say no, so I joined them. It was fun. We played, we drank. I wasn't drunk at all, but they all became very cheerful.

After midnight I chose to retire, but one of them followed me. I was careless, because I didn't lock my door immediately, and he entered. He started forcing himself on me, croaking that he loves me and wants me. I was petrified. I felt his hands all over me and his smell of smoke and alcohol made my stomach turn. He pulled me onto my bed, I could feel his heavy body falling on me. My heart was pounding from fear, I cried, desperately tried to free myself from his firm grip. I felt so disgusted, so ashamed, so dirty... The next moment I felt his grip loosening, which was followed by a deep snoring. He fell asleep. I carefully slipped out from under him. I didn't dare leave my room, I was worried about my valuables. I also feared that I'd bump into the other men and I wouldn't be so lucky with them. I crawled into a corner of the room, grabbed my pocket knife and waited until morning, without ever falling asleep.

Around seven a.m. he woke up, mumbled some apology about not remembering anything and being drunk. Then he left the room. I quickly locked the door after, and tiredly fell asleep. I swear I'll never talk about this to anyone. It's so shameful. I'm so grateful, I was so lucky! It could have been so much worse."

Elena's notes:

Trust your gut. This phrase proved to be truthful all my life. If you feel on a gut level that you shouldn't do something, shouldn't trust somebody, shouldn't say yes to a deal, then don't. I recall that night so many times, it was so shocking. I have traveled alone since then, slept on the beach, and met other blue-collar workers. I have never had that gut feeling of danger since that night.

This is a good illustration on how to try to be less judgmental at the wrong time. I read the stories of many high achievers, and very often encountered the sentence "trust your gut", "listen to your heart", and "believe your first instinct."

Exercise your gut skills. When you make a judgment, such as about a stereotyped group, your partner or others, listen to what your gut is saying.

"Do I judge based on what I learned or based on what I feel?"

It happens so often that we judge because we know we're supposed to judge. If we see a poorly dressed man, we instantly think that he's a dangerous outlaw. If our partner comes home late we immediately assume that he was doing something fishy. Why? Because we're conditioned to believe it so.

When I was a kid, my parents to guard me and drag me away from bad-looking people. When a man (or woman) gets home late, what's the first explanation you get from friends, television or stupid romance books? "Maybe he was seeing someone else..." BS. I can't tell you anything more on this. It comes from conditioning and accepting information without putting your own thoughts into it.

If you feel on a gut level that someone means harm, or your spouse was in the wrong, then take the action you find the most appropriate. If you feel that you want to behave like a cliché because this is how you think you're supposed to react, think about it again.

I could have been more careful, listened more to my first instincts and not get so familiar with those men. I should have just gone up to my room and locked the door. Or, when the guy fell asleep I could have called the police, I could have called the gatekeeper. Take a picture, complain to the house providing services – anything. But no, I decided that my shame was greater. I was okay with being abused and felt lucky that nothing more happened. What a naïve and carefree way of living life! However, the memory haunts me today. I forgave myself, and I'd do things differently now. It's just so hard to accept that valued myself so little back then.

"I went on a date with this guy I met on a dating site. It was our second date when he brought me home. He took me to the local bar, we played cards and drank with his friends. He couldn't drive me home and there were no buses, so he offered me his guest room to stay. Later that night he came in the room and forced himself onto me. He was much bigger than I and drunk. I kind of liked him so instead of resisting I tried to enjoy it, but I didn't. I felt so horrible afterward. I know is my fault, but I really think it was borderline rape. I didn't tell anyone about it, though. I was afraid and ashamed." (Eszter, 22, Budapest)

"It was our third date. Holy cow, that was one crazy woman. I took her to a restaurant, nice little private terrace. She drank and ate like it was the end of the world and I didn't want to pay all the bill. I paid on the previous two dates, and I didn't feel it fair. When we asked for the bill, I mentioned to her how she'd like to split it. She became very angry, started screaming with me being a cheap b..., poured the wine in my eyes, stole my sunglasses from the table and ran away. I never dared to talk about this with anyone before. I seem like a pussy and I'm ashamed that I let my guard down, but who the heck would expect something like this?" (Charles, 36, Singapore)

I hope these events are less frequent than I think they are, and not everybody experiences them, but they certainly can occur. You can't always prevent them. Using your gut instinct can be a good method, but many times it's not enough. If something bad happens, or almost happens, but you feel emotionally, physically or sexually abused, you shouldn't take it easy.

People who are abused in some way often think that they are alone. They are scared and often ashamed. Many women who are victims of domestic violence keep silent because they are terrified, or they feel they can't speak up because of religious beliefs, financial insecurity, or for the sake of their children. Men most often keep silent about abuse because of the shame they feel. They perceive that letting a woman or another man taking advantage of them is a sign of insufficient masculinity.

Each country has its own numbers and services for domestic abuse. The US has a National Domestic Violence hotline that people can instantly call. If an unexpected event happens, 112 or 911 can always be a good start to call for help.

I think it is very important to take action whenever we experience abuse for two reasons. The first reason is the obvious one – nobody has the right to offend our physical and mental integrity. It's unlawful, unethical and shouldn't go unpunished. The other reason is the peace of mind we get after we take action. Calling out for help and seeking justice for ourselves won't totally reverse things, but at least it will help our sense of self-respect and self-love.

On the other hand, if we do nothing, it will itch and harm our mind, we'll be frustrated about it and it will always stay with us as an unfair event, an injustice that went on without consequence. Our self-esteem will decrease. We will feel that we're destined to endure shame and pain. This won't help us have a happy life. We have to seek justice for ourselves because nobody else will. The very least we can do is tell friends and family about the abuse, regardless how ashamed we might feel, so they can help us seek justice if we can't.

It seems like good-for-nothing advice to say "get over your shame, it doesn't matter, just get over it." It's not easy. My mom, while healthy, and my grandmother were very religious and instilled in me the feeling of shame very deeply. It was not easy to get it out of my system.

Shame can be a very harmful negative emotion. We feel it when our actions differ from our beliefs and values. People's shame sensitivity is very different. It really depends on what we think is right or wrong. For example, a serial killer might not feel shame about killing somebody, but feel intense shame if they get caught. Not because they regret their actions, but because they weren't good enough to escape. On the other hand, if someone kills someone by accident, they don't feel any shame by being caught, they usually give themselves up. However, they feel eternal guilt and shame in taking someone's life – even if involuntarily.

This extreme example shows how differently people perceive shame in the same situation. This is why you never should compare your shame sensitivity with someone else's. Don't feel bad if you consider something shameful and someone else doesn't or vice versa. We are different.

There is, however, an unhealthy level of feeling shame where one should take action to diminish it. This unhealthy level starts when the feeling of shame starts sabotaging one's life, causes unhappiness and takes away their peace of mind. Shame is a very conscious emotion. We know that we're ashamed of something. It has physical symptoms (red cheeks, feeling the heat in our skin) and mental signs (low self-esteem, poor self-image). Feeling too much shame can lead to depression, addictions, eating disorders, or sexual disorders as a consequence. It is important to be dealt with.

Feeling shame as a teenager when being around the secret sweetheart is normal. Feeling ashamed (and guilty) for being late for a meeting is acceptable. Not taking action when being abused, or not standing up for ourselves because of shame is not okay. I think that shame can be considered exaggerated when we start sabotaging our lives because of it.

The way I started acting — and successfully overcame most of my shame issues — was quite simple. As I traveled, I started asking people about their experiences regarding shame. It was so fascinating to see how easily they opened up about their shame when talking to strangers. I could open up more easily, too. It was like a worldwide "anonymous ashamed ones" one-on-one session.

Hearing others' experiences, asking for objective standards and hearing how people in the same shoes cope with their problems help make us feel understood, not alone and most importantly less ashamed.

Practicing talking to strangers about our shame makes us feel more okay about them, more secure about ourselves, and confidence by overcoming a fear.

The feeling of shame clouds our better

judgment, we are too invested it the situation. Therefore, it is good to use someone else to think in our place.

There is a scientific testing technique used by psychologists researching shame to determine whether someone feels too much of it. The test is called Guilt and Shame Proneness Scale (GASP). Taking this test can be a good start to see where you stand on the guilt and shame scale. If your score is excessively different than "normal" and you feel that you can't cope with the result alone, you might want to reach out for the help of a specialist.

When it is not exaggerated, shame can be a good teacher. When we overstep our morals, the unpleasant feeling of shame and guilt can prevent us doing it again. For example, we say ugly things to our friend or partner because, let's say, we had a bad day at work. But when we cool down and analyze the situation we realize that our behavior was improper, and our actions were in opposition to our values of being a gentle person. We'll feel ashamed, and hopefully, say sorry. The unpleasant feeling of shame and guilt might prevent us doing the same mistake again. In this sense, feeling shame can be a good advisor in what's wrong or right and can help us correct our shortcomings.

In a relationship it is good to talk with your significant other about the things that make you feel ashamed. On one hand, if you open up about your deepest fears related to shame, it's a sign of trust towards your partner. It will be appreciated. On the other hand, knowing what the other's shame-boundaries are can help you being mindful of them. You can also talk about your shame issues to find a solution on them together.

Never use the shame card to win an argument. If your partner honestly opens up about his or her vulnerabilities, never try to use it against him or her. It's a nasty move that is unacceptable in a loving relationship. It will do a lot of damage – decrease trust, weaken your bond and deepen the sensation of shame in the victim. If you truly love somebody, you simply don't do that.

Chapter 6: Mood Swings

January 10th, 2006

"Today I met a man… well, not just any man. I can't even think about how to phrase this. It was so magical. The Sensei was talking about a man who is "veteran" in the karate group, and was on a one-month travel hiatus. Today he showed up. He was masculine, handsome, serious, mysterious, tacit and so focused on karate. No wonder, he's done it for eleven years. The Sensei paired me with him today, and I think he chose exercises that required a lot of body contact. The matchmaker… His name is Dimitri. Even his name is so masculine – what a man! I can't stop thinking about him… The karate movements, as he looked at me with his dark brown eyes – so intense. I should prepare a report for work tomorrow, but I simply can't focus. The only thing I can think about is how to wear my gi (classical karate clothing) to be more feminine in it."

12th January, 2007

"Dimitri didn't show up for today's class and I feel so disappointed. I feel literal physical pain in my chest. Why? Why do I care, anyway? Maybe he doesn't like me. He looks so confident and secure, and I'm just a newbie girl with an overly cheerful attitude. Maybe he thinks I'm childish. What type of girl does he like? I should act like that the next time he comes. Maybe I should be more distant... oh, I'm sure I will be as red as the Communist Manifesto when I see him. That's so childish! I'm a grown woman! I have to act accordingly."

14th January, 2007

"I met with the Sensei today. He told me that he talked with Dimitri and he thinks I'm pretty! I feel like I could run a marathon! I can't wait for tomorrow's encounter! I hope he comes!"

15th January, 2007

"He showed up for today's training, but I wasn't paired with him. Why did the Sensei do that? He knew how much I wanted to practice with him! I feel so disappointed. The only thing I can think of is that Dimitri asked the Sensei to pair him with someone more experienced, not a loser like me. Maybe the Sensei told me that Dimitri thinks I'm pretty to make me feel better. How disappointing. I'm sure he doesn't like me. Why do I care, anyway? I should focus on my report. I'm in a five-day delay."

January 25th, 2007

"Today I learned that Dimitri is in charge of managing the production section at his dad's company, and he often has to stay longer at the office. That's why he shows up so rarely for karate classes. It makes me somewhat relaxed. I thought he didn't come to avoid me. But why would he do that? I think I'm starting to have some serious judgment issues here, I hardly recognize myself. Even the behavior of my crazy, suicidal roommate doesn't seem so crazy anymore. I'd rather jump out of the window myself than to wait another day to see if Dimitri shows up for tomorrow's training."

January 26th, 2007

"Today we talked! And he came to me! This means something! He is definitely interested, and I did well to resist the temptation to initiate the conversation! He even invited me to a weekend event where veterans of the karate group gather for drinks. It will be the day before my birthday. Maybe he'll give me more attention or even a kiss as a present. I feel so very excited I can't put it in words!"

February 11th, 2007

"I don't even know from where to begin. The karate reunion was yesterday. We went out to a pub, drank, and played pool. Oh, the pool... I'm actually good at it, but I wanted to get him in the cliché trap of pretending of not knowing how to play. And he got hooked on it, so he walked behind me, leaned closer and positioned my hands in the right direction. I could feel his lotion, he smelled so good. I don't even know why I did this? Do I want to get a premature heart attack? At least I didn't need to pretend that I play badly. I couldn't even hit the ball straight, I was so nervous. When the distance grew a bit between us, I could focus again and win the game. Finally, I got his attention with something I'm good at! He constantly stood close to me, even put his arms around me. My heart was pounding so loud that I was afraid he might hear it. We had a very good time, met some of his old friends. When the fun was over he offered to take me home. He didn't drink all night to be able to drive safely. So responsible. By the time we got home it was past midnight. He told me happy birthday and kissed me… I'm at a loss for words. I felt that all the volcanoes existing on Earth erupted in me at the same time! I longed for this moment for an eternity!"

Elena's notes:

Oh dear, love is truly blind. I've fallen for him as

you can only fall for your first love: blindly and unconditionally. Back then I didn't know that what is even better than falling in love is rising in love. In Dimitri's case, falling was the right phrase. It was not a love without pain. In fact, being with him I experienced all the painful, torturing sides of love. I fell — deeper and deeper.

Is it a surprise, considering that my self-esteem at that time was equal to a discounted tomato in a Chinese shop? I made many mistakes right from the beginning. What's more, even before it even started, I was utterly unconfident, but I faked confidence. I made up lies, tried to rationalize everything that seemed fishy from the start.

There's a general law of the universe. Based on my experience, I can confirm that similar attracts similar. Dimitri and I were very similar considering our self-esteem. Both of us were faking it, making each other believe that we were so secure in ourselves.

It's normal, and a mistake committed more often

than one would think. Everybody wants to be as attractive as possible when a male or female awakens their interest. People lie, play roles, put on a mask that makes them seem invincible. But lies can't be sustained forever and the performance of their lives turns out to be a cheap off-Broadway show, and the invincible mask a one dollar E-bay camouflage. Fake.

Then people wake up, and start blaming the other: "You weren't like this at the beginning", "You told me that you would never scream at me", and so on. Change into the negative is painful, especially when love is still involved. When in love, we tend to turn a blind eye to the things that we don't like about the other. What's more, we sometimes say, "I'm so happy I'm getting to know him better. It was painful, but at least he's opening up. Isn't that the next level?" We lie even to ourselves.

There are things that will come up in a relationship as disagreements. People are not the same, after all. You can talk through them, and move on. You may not agree with your partner but you accept his viewpoint. These are usually small things, they don't and shouldn't make a difference. For example, whether or not he likes Metallica, or how he likes his eggs to be fried, or how she likes to drive. When I say role-play and mask I'm not talking about these things. I'm talking about the big things, the things that are deal breakers that were masked before for the simple reason to seem more attractive.

Some people lie with a nasty purpose, to seduce, deceive and ultimately to get into your panties or get it into their panties. These relationships don't last too long most of the time.
 There are liars, like Dimitri, who are frustrated, full of complexes and they don't want to show it to others. Therefore, they lie and live in a constant terror about whether or not their lie is credible enough. There is another type of liar, like I was: those who desperately need to be loved, who would lie about anything to get it, who are oblivious of the consequences. Very *carpe diem* in a twisted and unhealthy way. It sounds harsh, and took me time to admit it to myself. Otherwise, I would never have stepped out of that vicious circle of lies.

How do you spot who is lying to seduce you and who's lying to cover up some self-related problems? It's easy. The seducers lie about you, the other types lie about themselves.

For example, a seducer will say cliché things like "You're so special, you deserve the best, you're so beautiful that hurts, he'd do anything for you" – and here's the trap. He doesn't. He just talks but apart from words you hardly ever see actions. Even if you see actions, those are not so mind blowing. Does he take you out to the cinema on Wednesday? Wow, I'm impressed. Or, did he invite you to an expensive restaurant when he's a millionaire? Not such a big deal – for him. These are nice things, but not in balance with the words. It would be in balance with his words if he took you to the cinema during the Super Bowl, or took you to a pricey restaurant while being needy. These are "real" sacrifices. My point here is not about the activities, but the motivation before someone reads and puts my lines on a superficiality index.

Those who lie because of their lack of self-esteem or love are not so easily detectable as the seducers. They mildly compliment you, and they usually mean it if the compliment doesn't seem exaggerated. But, they lie about themselves. Since you don't know them well enough at that point of the relationship, you can't tell for sure if they are lying or not.

However, you can test it out. The first step is to check their body language while they speak. If they say they are confident with crossed arms, avoiding your gaze, there is a high chance they lie. Body language, intonation, speaking speed, consequent talking are all signs that can reveal some hidden truths if you're aware and mindful enough. I have read more than ten books about body language and how to detect liars, maybe because I'm paranoid, or maybe because I learned more from those books than in school. Since I now possess that knowledge, I get cheated and deceived much less. To me it's an invaluable asset.

The second step is to drop our fish into deep water – taking him or her in different companies. Introducing them to your friends, family, or any other circle of people can help you detect whether your partner is lying about their self-esteem. If they act differently in each circle, showing a face that they think is expected to be likable, it's suspicious, especially if they mentioned things before that contradict their current actions.

People who are okay with themselves, who truly trust their ability, are the same with everyone. They don't fear unpopular opinions – not even in front of you. They might not be adored in each circle, but they are trusted.

I think detecting lies – our own or our (possible future) partner's – is essential and crucial if we want to increase our chances to live in a healthy relationship. If one or both of us lie, that comes out as ugly and brings more misfortune and pain than the brief happy lies do. Honesty might keep the relationship from even happening, but isn't it better to know your incompatibility as soon as possible? Before time, emotion and hopes make the separation more difficult?

If you feel that you lie to your (possible) partner, can you identify with one of these three types of liars? *Seducer, lack of self-esteem liar,* or *the liar for love.* If you lie about money matters or about your past to seem more interesting, that's self-esteem lying, too. If you know that you lie, I strongly suggest pulling your stuff together, and figure out why you feel the need to lie. Then deal with it – preferably before entering into a relationship. It will bring only misery and more insecurities to you if you fall lower with someone.

Another way to make sure you're heading on the right path with your romantic life is to ask and *listen* to the opinion of those who you truly trust. If a colleague who you hardly ever talk with tells you that person is not good, don't listen. If your father or best friend tells you, at least try to listen to their reasons before you send them to the ninth circle of Hell. Try to stay rational and notice that others have *nothing* to gain by telling you their opinion about your relationship. They are just looking out for you.

You can try to look at your romance and your crush from an outsider's point of view. Look with different eyes and reevaluate how everything is going. Are you satisfied and happy? Are there improvements to be made? Those kinds of things. Please be honest with yourself. There is no sense in lying to yourself.

If you blind yourself and keep making excuses, you'll suffer until you can take no more. I feel that if only I had listened to that nagging voice in my head, and the wise words of my loved ones, I could have saved myself from a lot of pain.

People are not out to get you, or to attack you. They want you to be happy if they truly are your loved ones. They have nothing to lose either way if your significant other is a jerk or not. They'll still love you. And they'll wish he or she was good enough for you.

Chapter 7: When You Think You're Not Good Enough

February 14th, 2007

"Today is Valentine's Day. He gave me incense sticks and chocolate. So thoughtful and perfect. Later we went out for a movie, and what happened there was far from perfect. I never experienced such anger and disappointment before. It turned out that in the row behind us, by the grace of the most evil odds, sat his ex-perfect-girlfriend with her Barbie-like friends. Regina George and her gang, anybody? During the movie I hardly dared breathe, I felt that any movement I'd make would look awkward. The best, most laid back, I-don't-care posture I could come up with was the flawless imitation of a motionless pale. I felt so nervous that I felt if I drank or ate popcorn, it would stick on my throat and I'd start coughing like a sick goat and I'd be the lamest person ever, and he'd run back crying to his ex. I just got home and started crying. Why is life so unfair? I imagined his ex-girlfriend with the two also perfect friends next to myself with my only two friends here, my two roommates who... well, they are far from perfect. Oh, I want to cry even more now. I better sleep."

Elena's notes:

Vanitatum vanitas, vanity of vanities. So many stupid preconceptions and superficial idealizations... And how often we do it! We set our mind on something that's ideal, beautiful, good and worthy and thus reject everything that doesn't meet that concept.

In my vanity concept of my worth in 2007 was dictated by the latest fashion trends I could never meet. Beauty was branded clothing, nice hair, and makeup. Ideal was having friends who also fit under my umbrella of worthiness and beauty. Good was the normal and not out of ordinary. In shortly, I worshiped everything that I wasn't and what I didn't have because of a deep and utter dissatisfaction with myself. I had a total inferiority complex that was boosted with the perceived fear that Dimitri would judge me and look down on me based on the same parameters I looked down on myself.

I didn't have an inferiority complex because I didn't meet my imaginary ideal self. I had an inferiority complex, so I continuously constructed ideals that surely weren't similar to me as a person. This way I could constantly torture myself that I was not ideal. Since I didn't feel ideal, I didn't behave as someone who was ideal. I was full of spasms and always felt that whatever I did was awkward.

A relationship will feel it. Maybe not in the beginning, because for a little while we can pretend otherwise, but sooner rather than later our lack of self-contentment and inferiority complex will come to the surface.

And just to be clear, I repeat again, when we have such a deep inferiority complex, our negative thoughts don't make it grow. Our negative thoughts are the result of the inferiority complex.

For many years I thought that if I try to reduce my negative thoughts, I will feel less inferior. But it never worked out. I got caught up fighting tons of limiting beliefs, negative self-talks, but I failed and this sense of failure made the negative bubble even bigger. "She's better, she's more well-dressed, he'll go back to her. Why should he stay with you? You're a loser, you're a loser." These thoughts, like the news on the radio, invaded my thoughts multiple times a day. My fight against them was in vain. When I somehow forgot about them for a few hours, I felt weird and started thinking about what was missing from my day. "Oh, the negative thoughts I should overcome," but by remembering them they were back, and intruded more aggressively.

This is how I struggled through my relationship with Dimitri. But now, I finally cracked the code and figured out the solution. I wish I could scream it so loud to the world that everybody would hear it:

It's not about the negative thoughts, it's about

their root: the negative self-image. Not the small thoughts should be eradicated, but the mentality that triggers them.

Now, this doesn't seem like a breakthrough thought, but when you're caught up in an inimical fantasy world where you can't see clearly, and you feel that you live from self-hating thought to self-hating thought, this realization is like a light in a dark tunnel.

The key is to improve your self-image.

How?

By questioning each and every self-judging, negative thought you have. Don't fight them, question them. If you think, "his ex-girlfriend dresses up much nicer than I do", or "has cooler friends" just ask, "Does this really matter?" He left that girl for a reason in the first place. He didn't consider staying with her just because of her or her friends' looks.

If you don't feel encouraged enough by this thought, ask another question: "If he'd leave me for her looks, what kind of person would I truly consider him to be?" Be honest, don't answer this question with crazy affirmations like "I deserve to be dumped because I look like trash", or "He is right about choosing her because she's better." That's malarkey, those are not your honest thoughts. Those are easy thoughts, things you choose to believe out of negativist routines. These are the answers of a person tormented by an inferiority complex. However, know that your inferiority complex is nothing but a thought – and so are all the other negative feelings related to it. They can be changed any time.

Look deep inside your soul and realize that all of your perceived, fear-driven inferior thoughts have a basis. They only exist in your head. And if, in a one-in-a-million chance, they'd turn out to be true, it would prove that you don't lose much in the first place. If you answer your question truthfully, you'll realize that if your man leaves you for a pretty dress, or any other superficial reason, he wasn't worth your effort in the first place. Nobody does who trades humans for objects, and interior value for superficial splendor.

Focus on yourself. Work on getting rid of the inferiority complex. There is always a point in your life when you feel inferior to someone – sometimes for the most banal reasons, like having curly or straight hair. An inferiority complex is a subjective state of mind. It's based on your emotional self-image. Trying to explain it with emotional reasons won't help. If you practice some rational self-examination, you can often realize how ungrounded your inferiority actually is.

Find the reason first: why do we feel inferior in a situation or to a person? Is it because we could never live up to our parents' expectations? Is it because someone body-shamed us in the past? Don't think too much, just give the first reason that crosses your mind.

After finding the reason, narrow down whom are you feeling inferior to. "Everyone" is not an answer. Do we feel inferior to rich people or beautiful people? Maybe good public speakers or joke tellers? Or the exes of your current partner? When the people are identified, take out the objective card: why do you feel this way towards them?

When you start thinking of whys, you realize that the "reason" you identified before is not the real reason. For example, let's stick to my example. I felt inferior to Dimitri's ex-girlfriend because I felt that I wasn't as pretty as her. My first "reason" was the level of attractiveness, but the real reason was the fear of losing Dimitri to her. Another example: someone feels inferior to good public speakers. The first "reason" might seem to be that this person is bad at speaking in public, but the real reason is that he's afraid of what the listeners will think of him, and how harshly they will judge.

The best way to fight the real reasons for your inferiority complex is to ask yourself: "Is this happening now?" Whatever that fear, that tragedy you create in your head is just there, in your head. Look around, there are no clouds anywhere. You're not being shamed in public speaking, you're not getting dumped. Why live your life stressing about yourself for an event that didn't, and might never, happen?

We are all inferior to someone in some way, but we're superior in other ways. Everyone has their strengths and weaknesses. It's futile to create complexes. Don't try to thrive on comparison with others. Think about how you can make yourself the best you can be instead. Think of the positive ways you can make progress in your life and be happier, be better in the things you really care about. Just be the best version of the person you can be for your sake and the sake of your relationship.

Don't let your inferiority complex and your perceived negative thoughts stand in the way of your happiness. Shift the perspective, don't let thoughts like "he'll leave me because I'm not good enough", or "our relationship will end soon" scare you. Thoughts like that can make you scared and weak. If you tell yourself "he'd be stupid to leave me because I'm the best he ever had, he'll never forget me even if he leaves", these thoughts will empower you. So, stop complaining and start working on yourself.

The rule of questioning negative self-image, finding the real reason for your fears, and putting it into a rational context applies to every issue you face, not just appearance-related ones. I examined this process through my own example, but you can translate it to any issue you have with yourself – and your partner.

Chapter 8: Lies We Tell Out of Shame

April 14th, 2007

"We've been together for more than two months now. I met his parents, they were very welcoming. His mom always packs some dinner for me when he comes to training to make sure that I'm properly fed. She is almost like a mother to me, too. I feel very cozy when we go and visit his family. The only thing I'm afraid of is that he is becoming more and more impatient about sex. And I want him badly, but I am so ashamed that I'm still a virgin. A few days ago, in a weak moment I lied to him that I'm not. But now, how can I "revirginize" myself without becoming a liar? Why? Why did I lie? Why am I still a virgin? I'm seriously thinking of buying a vibrator and taking my virginity to solve this issue. But I'm afraid. I also want him to be the first, not a plastic banana."

April 21st, 2007

"I confessed my lie and he took it quite lightly. First, he didn't want to believe me, but then he told me that he hasn't had much experience with women, either. I was quite surprised, but thinking through how much he worked at his father's company and how devoted he was to karate, it made sense. I feel so relieved. I will never lie again about something like this. I don't even get why virginity is such a dividing topic. Some people think about it as something that should be kept until marriage. Others lose it at the age of fourteen and down-talk the confidence of those who still have it at my age. I think nobody should be judged by their sexuality-related decisions. Those who want to preserve it until marriage have the right to do so, it's their own body. Those who lost it early and regret it have enough pain to deal with. They lost something forever. People shouldn't mock them or point fingers. People like me should be left alone, too. The pressure and expectations of losing one's virginity can push us to do something extreme and regret it, or take our confidence even more and stay virgins out of shame. We don't get any younger, after all. I think the same applies to men. Dimitri seemed so bashful talking about it, too."

April 30th, 2007

"It happened! We had sex for the first time! It was an amazing experience! We both trembled, wanted it so much to happen. The timing was perfect, everything was like a fairytale. I'm so happy I waited and I gave my most unique gift to him. I feel that we both love each other very much, and first love on the first occasion can create magical bonds. He seemed very happy, too."

Elena's notes:

It was such a stupid lie. I made a trap for myself. I'm sure it affected Dimitri's trust in me later, even if it was a lie, which came out of shame. At that point neither Dimitri nor I was emotionally mature enough to discuss and accept this lie for what it was: an immature way of trying to seem more mature. Lies like this are harmful in a relationship because it decreases our credibility. It doesn't matter how innocent or fear-driven it may be.

When you try to sell someone a lie and you think it is innocent, always meditate on how would you react, or how innocent you might consider it if it came from your partner. Would you treat it as a nothing, or get worked up about the fact that your significant other lied? Would you weigh his or her reasons first, or the naked facts?

Relationships aren't that complicated. Just think about how would you feel or act if your partner did or said the same thing you're about to. If we used this one simple guideline in what we do or say to our partner, our relationship would be much harmonic, close to ideal.

Virginity really shouldn't be a thing you lie about. I hope not many people can relate to me in this aspect. If you're a virgin, your partner should feel honored on some level to be the first one with you. If you're not a virgin anymore, don't feel ashamed or weird either. It is just the way it is, and it's a condition that doesn't determine you as a person.

The media and Hollywood movies don't help. Social shame surrounding virginity is kept alive and heightened in films and TV shows, and they usually don't get a good angle on the topic. They make virginity a target for malicious humor. Don't fall for that. In fact, nobody cares as much about your virginity as you do. It doesn't matter to anyone else as much as it does for you, and this is an excellent reason why you should wait for the right person. In case you're a virgin, just for your own sake wait for the positive experience you deserve.

As it is, lying about virginity is just one of the many lies people tell at the beginning of the relationship.

> "My boyfriend was traveling with a girl before we met. He told me that she was his half-sister moving to Hong Kong for studies. He told me she was the 'love child'

of his dad's affair, so I never asked too much about the topic. Eight months later I thought I would ask how his sister likes Hong Kong when he finally confessed to me that she was not his sister, just a friend. But at that starting point of our relationship, it would have been awkward to confess to me that he was traveling with an unrelated female just days before he met me. I understand his point, but still. It took me time to trust him 100% again." (Allison, 26, USA)

Lies can root in different motivations. Allison's boyfriend probably meant no harm, and considering their circumstances there is sense of why he said what he did. He didn't know they'd get serious. During our conversation, Allison told me that her boyfriend was pretty direct and quick in admitting his lie once she asked about the "sister". That's why she believed that he just forgot about the business.

Forgetting your lies is another big danger that can bring misfortune on your head. A lie is not like a real experience that you felt with your own skin and thus you never forget. A lie is a patched up story in your mind. If you get into the habit of stacking small lies about yourself, you'll end up falling in your own trap.

If you already have told lies, admit them to your partner, be upright and quick. Apologize, be honest and then wait for your partner to decide to forgive or not. Honesty liberates the soul. Lies poison your mind and imprison you. The truth takes off your chains. Truly.

Chapter 9: How to Notice Early Mental Conditioning and Emotional Abuse

June 3rd, 2007

Dimitri told me that he loves how determined I am in the things I do, my free spirit and curiosity. And the bold way I act sometimes. I didn't consider myself particularly bold, but I guess since I lived alone for a while I became good at making decisions for myself without too much hesitation. My financial and lifestyle freedom made me stronger. I was happy with his remark.

July 2nd, 2007

Dimitri acts oddly sometimes, and I'd like to help him so much. The more I get to know him, the more I realize that he has a complicated relationship with his father. Both are alpha male types, but his father is the senior and still treats him as an oblivious kid. I feel this disturbs him a lot. I'm sure I'm over-thinking it, but he often takes his anger out on me. He tells me that I don't know anything about patronizing parents since I don't have to deal with them. His remarks hurt me, but he is right. He is in a very dependent situation.

August 10th, 2007

Today we came back from a three-day wellness trip. I have mixed feelings about it. We went to the seaside, amazing view, sun, surfing – all you can imagine paradise to be like. I complimented Dimitri on his flawless body, but he rejected my compliment. He said he looks like a piece of crap. I have no idea why he does this. He talks about himself in such a mean manner sometimes, and it hurts me. I love him and I'd like to help him feel better about himself so much, but he always pushes me away. On the last day of the trip he even told me that I shouldn't show myself so eagerly to other men on the beach in that small piece of a napkin I call swimsuit. I only wanted to show myself off to him so he would like me more. I spent almost half of my salary on this swimsuit, but I felt it was worth it. I thought he'd like it. He apologized later, but I still feel bad about it. He totally misunderstood the situation.

September 12th, 2007

"Summer was chaotic, but I feel autumn starts to chill things out. Dimitri has more free time now, so we spend a lot of time together. We stay at his place mostly. He has an entire floor to himself at their family house. His dad often asks me to do the chores and help with smaller tasks around his business, but I don't mind. I technically live there now. Often I go to work from there in the morning. The least I can do is to do the chores. I actually have a good relationship with Dimitri's father. Sometimes I feel that he dislikes it. But that's just my imagination.

Elena's notes:

The bubble of imagined strength and self-confidence started to blow out on both of our sides. He started to show signs of severely damaged self-esteem, and I started to become more and more controlled by his moodiness. I desperately tried to cheer him up, giving compliments and saying kind words. The only person from whom he expected positive feedback was his dad who gave only disparaging words, and he couldn't identify with my high regards of him. As a result, he rejected me again and again.

I'm still not sure why, but he found exquisite pleasure in seeing me desperate. Rejecting my compliments made me desperate, but after a time I learned that it was better to show my love in different forms than words. Then, he started down-talking himself to me to make me desperate again. I couldn't control his actions, so this game persisted throughout our relationship.

Sometimes I thought I'd break his game, replying, "Yes, you're a pile of crap." At that time I didn't realize agreeing with him would drag me into an even deeper and nastier mind game of his. I can't count on my two hands how many times we played this. When I agreed with him, he countered it by saying, "Yeah, I knew it, thank you for being finally honest." And he made me a liar, a faker, he even broke up with me sometimes. He made me so scared that I burst out crying, apologizing for whatever I had done just to prevent him from leaving me.

When I write these lines years later, I know now that it was so wrong, so messed up. I'm almost stunned how I didn't notice it earlier. How could I fall prey to this vicious mind game again and again? Yet, I did. It was normal back then. I thought that this is what a relationship meant. He convinced me that this was what I created, and I couldn't get anything better. This was the type of relationship I was destined to live in, and he accepted me despite it all.

This is why I beg you, who read my lines, don't ignore the signs. If you can relate to anything from my experience — especially in the case of abuse — do something about it. It is NOT NORMAL. I know better than anyone that it seems normal while in the dark bubble. Sometimes you feel deep down that you shouldn't be in that relationship, that you should leave and you deserve better. The guilt that shortly follows these thoughts will overshadow any reason.

Emotional abuse and emotional manipulation are very dangerous for two reasons. The first reason, the obvious one, is that the abuser can do a lot of damage to the receiver's self-esteem and self-worth. In severe cases, an abuser won't stop at emotional abuse but will use physical and mental terror, too.

The second reason why emotional abuse is dangerous is that while you live in the bubble, it's undetectable. It sneaks into your life in such an uncanny manner that by the time it should be obvious, it has become routine. Therefore, you consider it as normal.

During my travels and talking with other people I became familiar with other faces of emotional abuse.

> "My ex-wife was a very good emotional manipulator. She was — is — an incredibly skilled liar. Her favorite game was insisting on incidents that didn't happen when they did, and vice versa. Also, she told me

something one day, and another day she said she didn't say that. The problem was that she told me these things so convincingly that I ended up questioning my own sanity. She made me believe that the cause of the problem was just a part of my imagination. To her, it was a mean and smart way of getting out of trouble."
(Markus, 39, Vienna)

"My dad triggers my guilt to his advantage all the time. If I mention something I'm not okay with, he makes me feel guilty for mentioning it. Like the last time I told him that I don't want to pay a third of their bills since I don't live home anymore. He started telling me in teary eyes how little do they have, and how hungry he was the other day. If I don't mention something, he makes me feel guilty for keeping it to myself for so long. Either way, I'm at fault."
(Rohit, 28, New Delhi)

"My sister should get a statue for being the best victim ever. Nothing is ever her fault. No matter what she does — or doesn't do

— it's someone else's fault. Someone else forced her, or tricked her to do it. When I got mad at her, it was my mistake for having too high expectations of her. When she got angry, it was my fault for annoying her. She never could be held accountable for anything. She's my younger sister, so in our childhood I had to suffer a lot because of her temper. Now I just try to avoid her as much as possible." (Grace, 41, Melbourne)

November 30th, 2007

"I didn't write for a long time, but I feel that I must do it now. I feel so hurt, and I know I'm crazy, and Dimitri didn't mean any harm, but I still took it on my soul. The other day, apparently a female colleague of his (his ex-girlfriend's Barbie friend) saw us together and told him that he set the bar very low with me. Dimitri told me that he considered this complete nonsense, and that the girl was out of her mind. But was this information really that necessary to share? Now I feel that his colleagues, his ex, and friends are bad-mouthing me about how I look behind my back. I know I don't dress as fashionably since I'm not a millionaire, but I don't think I'm a last resort either. I can't think of any other reason Dimitri told me this other than that he doesn't like my style, and he wanted to tell me in a roundabout manner, probably to hurt me less."

Emotional manipulators can bring you to very low and dark places, undermining your sense of self. They can make you doubt your own sanity, as in Marcus' case, or they can target your weak spots. Dimitri was an expert in hitting me where it hurt the most. I was insecure about my style and looks, and that's why he casually mentioned the story about his colleague that he could easily just forget without telling me. He was bitterly aware emotionally, but he used his knowledge to make me feel worse.

However, like any other human interaction, emotional abuse and manipulation is bidirectional. You can't be manipulated if you don't enter into their games. It all happens with your consent and cooperation. This is the painful truth. This is my painful truth. Dimitri did what I enabled him to do. I didn't say no or stop. Or, when I did, I wasn't persistent and consequential with my threats, so all I achieved was to undermine my own credibility.

How does one handle emotional manipulators?

First, I recommend that you stay as far away from these people as possible. It really doesn't matter if they are friends or family when their behavior is unhealthy. If they make you feel guilt, insecurity, undermine your intelligence, sabotage your sense of self-worth, that's a clear red light to start keeping some distance. You have to choose yourself first.

Another thing I've learned on my own, and from the tales of others, is that emotional manipulators hardly ever change. Even when they do, that won't happen because of the nice words of the person they manipulate. They may come to their senses due to some sort of negative shock, like a breakup, or an empty family table at Christmas. However, you shouldn't feel guilt because of them. It's not your duty to save them and spend your life energy on it.

If you can't avoid emotional abusers and manipulators, there is another way to shut them out. They are annoying because whatever they do or say is so irrational, and truly go against any reason. Don't try to play their games. Don't respond to madness with madness. As soon as you enter their field, they'll overwhelm you with their experience. Quit trying to beat them at their own game.

Distance yourself from them emotionally. This is the most difficult part, but the only way to go. I honestly think that someone who has never suffered emotional abuse or manipulation can't do it. You must know how painful and harmful emotional abuse is to be able to keep distance emotionally from a loved one. With enough awareness and willpower, you'll succeed. Approach them more like they're a science project. Respond only to the facts.

If we're talking about emotional manipulators who are not so close to you, it's much easier to distance yourself. If it's your birthday and someone still finds a way to make the day only about her or himself, that's not normal. These people begin their attention scavenger hunt with small actions, like interrupting you or talking over you. If they don't get the attention they crave, they become unnecessarily loud or obnoxious, their actions can even take a more drastic turn, such as starting arguments. The world should not rotate around one person. The best action you can take is to pay little or no attention to them. Otherwise, they'll have an audience and will feel even more encouraged to talk about themselves.

If you have tried to distance yourself emotionally but still find yourself making excuses for your manipulators' behavior, or compromising your own choices to please them, seek help. The negative feelings regarding a situation may not instantly appear, but may arise later when you revisit the situation. If you think a conversation through and the emotions of guilt, inadequacy, or fear emerge, it is time to take the issue seriously.

Speak with a counselor or a psychologist first to confirm your suspicions about the abusive person, whether the abuser is a partner, family member, or friend. Then, check with the specialist to learn the best next step in your case. Is your relationship still savable? Should you take immediate action to distance yourself completely? Each individual case is different, therefore they need to be addressed differently, but they need to be addressed.

Chapter 10: Codependency

December 24th, 2007

"I'm home. Dimitri left just yesterday to spend the holidays with his family. He came to visit my family for the first time. Everyone liked him. I'm so glad that my family has such a good opinion about him. My dad especially likes him for his martial arts passion. My dad did karate as well, they had lots of things to talk about."

January 20th, 2008

"It has been almost a year since Dimitri and I have been together. I hope we'll have fifty more! There have been ups and downs, but I feel it's worth it. The only thing I don't like is his constant self-torturing attitude. He doesn't want to accept my words of affirmation, but if I don't say anything he says I don't care. I don't find it fair. I care and would love to care more, but he simply doesn't let me. I feel so dumb. I'm sure there's a solution to help him, I just haven't figured it out yet."

February 8th, 2008

"He had a fight with his father yesterday. I don't think either of them was right or wrong, so I didn't voice my opinion. They were screaming so loudly I was scared they'd start a fight. When Dimitri came up to the room he smashed his wardrobe's door with one hit. I felt so terrified. I've never seen him so angry. I withdrew for a while to let him cool down. I was so surprised – it was not the cool, tacit Dimitri I got to know. After an hour I went into his room and asked him how he felt. He replied quite violently. He said, "How do you think I feel? How exactly? Like a stupid loser! Why does it always have to be his way? I hate living here!" I felt frustrated. I desperately tried to come up with something helpful and smart. I cautiously asked him something I had wanted to know for a long time. "Why don't you move?" I'm not sure what I said wrong, but he became very angry again. He said some horrible things about me being oblivious and stupid, and that he didn't want to end up living like me. This hurt a lot. I felt I worked hard and was independent. Later he apologized."

April 12th, 2008

"We moved out! We are renting a small but cozy studio! I really hope Dimitri will feel better here. The last few months were very hectic. I'm really concerned what to say to him, always thinking twice before opening my mouth. But somehow, when I tell him my three-times-proof thought phrases, he finds something disturbing in them. I think I became too cautious with what I say. It's my fault. Hopefully, everything will get better now."

May 20th, 2008

"It's been exactly two months since we moved out. We are doing very well now! We haven't had a fight for a month! He brought me flowers today and told me he loves me. I feel so cherished. He even gave me a foot massage, and we went out to see a movie in the evening. No disturbance this time. It's been quite a while since we did something together. "

June 1st, 2008

"I feel so helpless. Today Dimitri told me that we have nothing in common, he can't talk with me about anything, I'm ignorant, and I can't understand him. I don't understand where this came from. He also said that he feels like he's suffocating living in the same flat with me, going to karate with me. He needs more time to go to work now, and he doesn't have time to meet his friends. I'm sure it's my fault. I nagged him recently to go somewhere together – that's when he came up with the idea to go to the cinema. I didn't think it was unreasonable since we hadn't done anything together for almost a year – only staying at home, helping his dad, working, and going to karate class. I never told him to not meet his friends, in fact, I encouraged him. It really hurts me that he thinks I'm not a good conversationalist. I must get better."

June 25th, 2008

" Today he told me that he despises and looks down on people who don't understand his jokes. Yesterday he told me that I never get his jokes. Should I read something between the lines?"

Elena's notes:

I wasn't familiar with the concept of codependency when I was co-depending on Dimitri. I perceived that there was nothing wrong with my attitude towards him, I just loved him too much. By the time I became co-dependent, my self-esteem was already pretty damaged.

Codependency as a word is used in a very casual way, especially recently. The clinical definition of this word is the inability to tolerate the discomfort of others. Codependency isn't restricted to romantic relationships. It can be applied to all the relationships we have. It means we're constantly preoccupied with how others think or feel about us. We put others' well-being and needs in front of ours.

Codependency can grow into a pathological form. We become so preoccupied with others' problems, we want to help them or save them so much that we don't realize our kindness turns into malice. Ultimately, we start being resentful towards them.

I know for sure that I wanted to help Dimitri with his self-hating attitude, but the more I tried, the more he rejected me. I was angry with him, I was angry with myself. I blamed myself. I thought that the problem was not with him but with me. I wasn't the one who couldn't come up with a good way of convincing him of his worth. Codependency can create bidirectional resentment that poisons the whole relationship. This is why I feel that it's very important to consider codependency as a reason when examining what's wrong with our romantic or everyday relationships.

There are different types of codependent behavior. Some show codependent traits only when in a romantic relationship. Others have their brain wired with these traits, affecting each area of their lives. Codependent thinking doesn't have a cure, there is no magic pill that makes it go away. However, with awareness and mindfulness it can be shut out.

Why do people develop codependent behavioral patterns? The reasons can be many, but shortly speaking, the origins can be traced back to childhood. Growing up with a narcissist, with an alcoholic, a gambler, a maximalist parent, being the middle child, or without a parent are just a few reasons. Codependency is developed as a survival mechanism to get attention.

If you don't get the care and attention you need as a child, this may seem the only way to be happy. For example, let's say your dad was an overachiever and he wanted you, as his only child, to accomplish the dreams he couldn't. He constantly pushed you towards the basketball scholarship you were not interested in, but you wanted him to love you so badly. Since you noticed that you only got appreciation and attention from him when you did well on the court, you accepted your fate to aim for the scholarship even if you didn't want it. Subconsciously, it became natural to you to do things you didn't want to make others happy. You have empirical proof of how to do it.

The most common symptoms of codependent behavior are low self-esteem, people-pleasing, poor boundaries, obsessions, and denial, among others.

By poor boundaries I mean feelings, needs, and thoughts. Codependents feel responsible for others' feelings and problems. They tend to blame their own on someone else. In other cases, their boundaries become rigid, making it hard for other people to approach them.

Codependents can become obsessed when they think they've made a mistake. Sometimes they start fantasizing about ideal scenarios how they'd like things to be, instead of how they are, to avoid the pain of the present. This is a form of denial, which is also a common sign of codependence. They deny their feelings and needs. If they don't understand or know what they're feeling, they become focused on others' feelings instead. The same thing goes for their needs.

How can you recognize if you're in a codependent relationship? If your sense of purpose in life feels like making extreme sacrifices to satisfy your partner's needs, there's a chance that you're codependent on him or her. If people around you often point out that you're too dependent on each other that can be a sign as well.

If you feel that you can't cope with codependency alone, seek out a specialist. A counselor can help you identify your codependent tendencies. With help you will understand why you adopted this behavior in the first place. Together you'll work out methods to help you heal and transform old patterns. Practices for overcoming codependency include self-care improvement, better boundary setting, learning to help others in a productive way, like volunteering.

What do you do if you realize that you're in a codependent relationship? To fix a codependent relationship, the first step is to set boundaries. You need to find your individuality again. Do things that make you happy as a person. You can also talk with your partner and try to find mutually beneficial solutions, like doing things and setting goals that satisfy you both.

Reconnect with your old friends and family. Keep to an agenda, and schedule at least five meetings per week with five different people in the beginning of your anti-codependency campaign. Find new hobbies. Let it be an individual hobby. You know, each relationship needs breathing time, otherwise you'll never have something exciting and new to share.

Chapter 11: Dealing With Aggression

July 4th, 2008

"We had a horrible fight today. I had enough of his arrogant attitude towards me. Maybe I stepped over a line. He told me that I couldn't survive without him, I needed him, because without him I couldn't keep my own apartment, I needed his guidance in life. I should only look on my simplistic job to see how incompetent I am. I felt this was it, I couldn't bear it any longer. I told him that I thought he was mean and took his frustrations out on me. This is when all hell broke loose. He started screaming that he always knew that I pitied him and looked down upon him. That I always lied when I said something good about him to make fun of him. He pushed me against a wall and started hitting it with his fists. I was terrified and petrified. I felt that I couldn't move. When he backed off, I ran into our room crying, locked the door and started packing my bag. He hit the door violently. I feared he might smash it. Then, suddenly everything went quiet. I heard him cry, he sounded like he was chuckling. He desperately apologized for his behavior. It sounded so heartbreaking. I went out and opened the door. We talked through the evening about all the things we would like to change. We made peace. He promised it would never happen again."

Elena's notes:

When we talk about aggression it sounds so easy to recognize. How can it be defined? What is considered acceptable aggressive behavior, and what falls into the category of violence? Is aggression acceptable when someone is angry or frustrated and says things that he or she later regrets? Can violence be summarized as the use of physical force and injury to a person? Where is the thin line that separates "harmless" aggression from aggression that should be taken seriously? What was it in my case? He didn't hurt me, but for the first time, I was seriously afraid for my physical integrity.

I truly wanted to understand the nature of aggression and whether or not I was a real victim in those moments, so I read as many definitions for aggression as I could.

"Hostile aggression occurs when the aggressive behavior is aimed solely at hurting another, in other words aggression for the sake of aggression." (Buss, A. H. (1961) *The Psychology of Aggression*)

"A forceful action or procedure (such as an unprovoked attack) especially when intended to dominate or master." (Merriam-Webster. (1828) Dictionary and Thesaurus)

"Overt, often harmful, social interaction with the intention of inflicting damage or other unpleasantness upon another individual." (Wikipedia)

Neuroscientists have done a great deal of research to link aggression to different brain functions. It turns out that the "aggressive instinct" can be inherited, but it can also be a learned behavior.

When it comes to a relationship, I think, it doesn't really matter what the biological, scientific explanation for your partner's aggressive behavior is. As long as he or she does something that triggers such great fear in you that you fear for your physical or mental integrity (or for your life) that can be considered as aggression.

Don't try to find explanations for their behavior. Also, "don't take anything personally…What others say and do is a projection of their own reality…When you are immune to the opinions and actions of others, you won't be the victim of needless suffering." (Miguel Angel Ruiz)

When an aggressive, intimidating, or controlling person keeps you in fear, doesn't respect your boundaries, and tries to manipulate you with harsh and theatrical actions, and won't stop even when you ask them, deploy consequences. To assert consequences and hold yourself to them is one of the most effective responses you can have to cool off an aggressor. The consequence should be well defined and in balance with the harm done.

For example, if your partner is trying to suppress your opinion, you can tell that he or she won't listen and consider your side, you'll leave the conversation. If the aggressive behavior doesn't change, keep yourself to your word and leave the room for five to ten minutes. Let your partner reconsider their actions, and talk about the issue when they are willing to accept your side, too. Threatening with a breakup in this situation is out of measure (unless it happens unbearably often).

In my case with Dimitri, threatening with a breakup was not out of proportion. But, I should have kept myself to my word the next time it happened. Because it did happen, many times, and my consequences transformed into empty threats.

When you inform your aggressor of a

consequence, be consistent about it. If your consequence is out of proportion, chances are high that you won't respect them. You'll turn into a verbal aggressor yourself, and one who shouldn't be taken seriously. "I'll never cook to you again if you keep on being so pushy about when I should cook dinner." This is a threat out of proportion, bully vs. bully.

If your consequence is too mild, your aggressor won't stop his behavior. This is why you should be mindful when you choose to reply to aggression with a consequence. Be proportional and consistent. With the right boundaries set, your partner's aggression will eventually transform into respect. Keep in mind, this applies to partners who are not violently aggressive and don't threaten your mental, emotional or physical safety.

If the aggressor is someone not as close to you as your spouse, like a boss or a relative, the best you can do is ignore them. Not all controlling people are worth wasting time and energy on. Your time is more valuable than cornering them with witty comebacks. Your happiness and well-being are the most important. Keep a healthy distance and avoid engagement unless you absolutely have to. Even then, keep your cool and stay composed. Bullies are like bulls – if your head gets red out of anger, they will attack. If you keep your calm in front of them, they will look for another target.

If you decide to react to an aggressor's behavior, prepare for a more intense change of opinion. Aggressors usually are not reasonable. Without losing your cool, you have to pass the ball back to them. For example, they point their finger at you, telling you that your solution to solve a problem was rubbish. Instead of starting to defend your solution with reasonable arguments, ask how they would have handled the situation. If they are so certain about you being wrong, surely they have a better solution. Most of the time, they don't, so they will shut up. You have to pass the ball back, especially if their aggressive statements are unfair. If you show signs of intimidation, or you keep the "bully ball" on your side of the court, they will become more and more aggressive.

This is why the best you can do is ignore them. If

you choose to engage, you must outsmart them in bullying. Fortunately, it's not usually difficult.

In my case with Dimitri, hitting the wall and cornering me was on the brink of heavy aggression and domestic violence. In that case, answering the bullying with outsmarting him would not work. Unless I started to hit the wall harder than he, I couldn't have done anything directly to make him stop his behavior. That physically manifested aggression could have turned into anything. If you experience something similar don't pick a fight.

Recognize when you're in danger. It is important to be aware that such kind of rage and the violent manifestation is not in your aggressor's control anymore. How do you recognize that the aggression you face is dangerous? Abrupt, out of nowhere, extreme, out of proportion, screaming, irrational actions, and hitting objects are all signs of aggression getting out of control. They are unpredictable and this exhibits the danger category quite well.

You're still not injured, but there is a good

chance you could be. Don't forget that injuries are not only the physical ones. Calling you names, emotional blackmailing, body shaming are just as unacceptable as physical aggression.

If you have identified your aggressor being dangerous, let somebody close to you know about it. You can never know when it might benefit you that someone knows, understands your situation, and can instantly take action when you cry for help. If you're experiencing domestic violence, don't call your acquaintance, instead call a domestic violence hotline, or 911 (or 112 in Europe).

Take precautions and choose a place where you can go if you need to escape after a more serious fight. Be prepared that explosive fights can happen at any time, even at night. The place you choose to go and the person you choose to contact should be available to you at all times.

If you have children and you feel that your situation indicates they should be informed about your spouse's behavior, or about a possible "escape adventure", do the necessary precautions. Make an escape plan with them. You can even practice getting out of your home with them. Make sure they won't tell to your spouse about these plans since children don't always understand why adults do the things they do. If your child tends to complain about you to your partner if you don't buy a toy or chocolate, you should consider how many details you share with him or her.

What if you are the aggressive partner?

If you know that about yourself, it is already a great start. Awareness is the first step towards healing. I spoke with many people who admitted that occasionally they could act aggressively and were very impulsive.

"When I had impulsive, aggressive episodes, I felt overwhelmed. I just couldn't think or behave calmly or rationally. I needed to express my anger, I had to let it out. I was angry at my husband for being so calm and collected. I hated that I couldn't be like him. Why? Why do I have to be this train wreck? My aggressive behavior slowly strained my personal relationships. That's why I decided to go to a therapist. I only benefited from it. I understood the root causes of my anger. With her help I learned how to recognize and control my aggression." (Ruth, 37, Nurnberg)

Fast, shallow breathing, rapid heart rate, involuntarily clenched fists or jaw, difficulty to control thoughts, are all signs of rising tension. If you catch yourself in this moment, there is a chance that you can turn your anger around. Pay attention to what triggers your anger. Avoiding these situations can also help you gain control. Talk with a counselor about what should you do when you start feeling angry. Make a note about these triggers on your phone, or carry a notebook to write them down. When you feel that anger invade your brain, take out your notes, remind yourself of the exercises and start doing them.

There is a difference between normal anger and rage. A therapist will be able to tell you whether or not your anger is abnormal, and if so, what can you do to control it.

Chapter 12: Jealousy

September 15th, 2008

"The past few months were eventless. I am busy with work. Dimitri decided to go for a job in the capital, and I want to follow him, so I have to try to get a job there, too. Already sent out some CVs, hopefully, I'll get a reply. Recently a feeling of anxiousness stalks my mind. This has been going on for a while now, but now it starts to become devastating. I feel a deep fear of losing him. I don't want him to leave me. Recently he is more distant, we have sex just as a compulsory activity of couples. What would I do without him? After a year and a half, he became part of my life in every sense of the word. There is not always sunlight, but other relationships are not better either. There is my ex-roommate, for example, she had even more fights with her boyfriend than we do. And they are still together. I wish we would have fewer fights, though. Each week there is something, but I already consider that normal. I think it's normal. Somehow I already expect the fight coming. If five or six days go by without a fight I already expect it. Maybe I trigger it with this mentality, but indeed, one never fails to break out. Sometimes I feel that I'm bored and the fights are the only interesting, or rather let's say emotional, event in my life. But, I feel such remorse saying these things. Of course, I'm not bored with him! I'm just tired, I better sleep."

October 30th, 2008

"Today I wanted to surprise Dimitri at his workplace, but before I entered the building I saw him cross the street with a blonde woman. They must have had a very good conversation since they were laughing loudly. I never felt the sensation I felt before when I saw them. My heart squeezed into the size of a bitter seed, my stomach was bouncing and I felt deep hatred toward that woman even though I didn't know her. Is this jealousy? He never smiles and laughs with me like that. I feel so angry, so resentful! I do so much for him, I want to make him happy. Get up early, make his favorite food for breakfast, clean, I go a beautician to keep myself nice, I spend all my money on nice clothing so none of his colleagues bad-mouth me again. This is the reward? He's flirting with other women in ways he never does with me. I can't bear this!"

October 31st, 2008

"It is my fault. I was too worked up about that woman. But I didn't start angrily, I think. As soon as I mentioned to him that I saw him with a blonde woman he became very aggressive. He started screaming that I was sick, I was spying on him, making up stories, surely I didn't love him. I didn't want him to get away with his regular tactics of twisting the blame and making me apologize in the end. So, I spoke up uncommonly harshly and told him that I didn't like that he seemed happier with her than with me. He told me that she was much funnier, I'm psychotic, stupid, boring and overly dependent. I told him that he made me so! He took away all my confidence by constantly telling me that I wasn't able to do anything without him, with the never-ending fights where I always had to apologize, and making me feel stupid and ignorant all the time. Then, I'll never forget this for the rest of my life. He took out a knife. I froze, my heart skipped a beat, I thought he was going to kill me. But he put the knife to his throat instead and he screamed out loud that I would kill him if he did all these with me. If he is so bad that I should kill him! I fell into a hysterical daze, feeling all the power leave my legs. My mind went blank. I could see a little drop of blood trickling down his throat. I lost control, fell on my knees, started crying, apologizing, begging him to just stop. I told him that I was wrong, I was just angry, that it all was my fault. He finally released the knife. He held me and told me that it was okay. I feel like it's not okay at all."

Elena's notes:

As it later turned out, he was indeed cheating, but this is secondary now.

The emotion of jealousy is one of the most

useless one, and the most poisonous. It is not an individual emotion. It is usually triggered by another negative emotion, which is the real reason why people get jealous. These negative emotions can be fear, anger, sorrow, loss, envy, betrayal, inadequacy, and humiliation. I think the best you can do when you feel jealous is to think of what the negative feeling is that triggered your jealousy.

In my case, it was fear of loss and inadequacy. I felt that I wasn't good enough, I didn't make him laugh like that, and of course losing him terrified me.

There are other types of jealousies you can feel when in a relationship, like envy if your partner is more successful in something. You can feel humiliation and rage if your partner is treating their colleagues or friends better than they treat you.

Pay attention to how your body manifests when you feel some negative emotions. Fear feels like a dropping or clutching sensation in your chest and stomach. It mostly triggers the flight reaction. Anger is a burning, tight sensation in your head and arms. You feel ready to fight.

Jealousy has many faces, but all these faces can be broken down to one big issue: self-hatred or low self-esteem.

All the negative emotions that trigger your jealousy root in a poor self-image. People who consider themselves worthy and good enough don't get jealous. That type of person has a strong sense of self-respect and boundaries, and if their partner oversteps those lines, instead of feeling jealous and desperate, they clearly communicate what displeased them, and acts consequently if the behavior doesn't cease.

Improving self-image takes a lot of time. However, it is a good start if you raise your self-esteem by not lashing out whenever you feel jealous. Try to internally rationalize the feeling. When you have the real reason why you feel jealous and it still seems justifiable to speak about it, then ask your partner in a normal, cool tone. Anger and finger pointing will never bring you the desired results.

Why?

If you're wrong, your partner will rightfully feel accused and untrusted. This can escalate, and in the end they'll wind up doing the things you're accusing them of. Why stay good when he or she is condemned anyway?

If you're right and your partner has something to hide, a direct attack will elicit a direct defense as a response. They will deny whatever you say instinctively. Later, they will "hide the tracks" so your chances will decrease in finding out the truth. Also, it's possible that they will try to put the blame on you, say you're jealous, unfair, they'll wake up the guilt in you, and at the end you'll end up apologizing.

However, if you ask the right questions in a calm manner they won't immediately feel attacked, and they won't be as defensive. If they don't sense danger, it's possible that they'll say things that can help you detect a lie in their story — if there is any.

Take my case, for example. If I approached the

situation differently, I might have gotten different results. I had an advantage – I saw Dimitri with the girl, but he didn't know that. I could have just asked casually about his day, his work and colleagues and see what he would say. If he confessed anything about his female colleague without hesitation, that would have made me a bit more relaxed since he was not hiding it.

It's not a guarantee that he is not cheating, of course, just like the old saying, "Just because you're paranoid doesn't mean they aren't after you." However, at least it's an honest move. Also, I can exclude some fears before I investigate more about the situation.

If he hid it, that's still not a confirmation. It can be so insignificant to him that he really forgot to mention it. But, I could make a mental note about it and investigate further by asking questions and being more aware. However, just like in criminal law, everybody is innocent until proven guilty.

Even if it is difficult, you should stay calm when

you sense jealousy and be smart about it. Don't assume the worst about your partner instantly. Imagine how you would feel if your partner constantly assumed the worst of you. That's always a good way of thinking yourself out of actions that may harm your relationship.

If you can't help it and feel you must assume the worst, it means that trust is seriously broken between the two of you. If this is the case, think about whether or not your relationship has a chance for a better future. If you already know that you won't be able to trust your partner, and assume the best of them, and trust them, you have to seriously consider seeking a way out of it. Without trust no relationship can be happy and functional.

Jealousy, however, has many faces, as I mentioned before. It's not always about cheating and fear of loss. It can be envy, for example. You can be envious of your partner's successes. That's very harmful to a relationship, too, especially because in this case your partner is innocent. The issue is only in your head, and you have to sort it out yourself.

Don't mention it to your partner until you can specify exactly what you are jealous about and *why* do you feel that way. It can be challenging to admit that you have these feelings to your partner and even yourself. You can be tempted to find a reason to blame your partner about it. Please don't do that. Don't blame yourself, either. Envy is a normal feeling, and unless you let it escalate, it can be overcome quite easily.

Be compassionate with yourself. Think about a cause for your emotions. You might feel them because you don't want to lose your partner for "not being enough." Perhaps you lost a partner for this reason in the past. Bad experiences, mixed with the thought of the loss and a sense of inadequacy, can create shadows where there aren't any. Don't punish your partner for something he or she is not guilty about.

Write down all your thoughts and experiences about your envy, understand them, and forgive yourself for them. Then, if you think it would help, share them with your partner. Tell that you love them, and you know that they are not at fault, but to seek help you'd like to share some thoughts with them. Tell them why do you feel envious, talk about your previous experiences. Mention your real fears regarding this feeling – probably the fear of losing them because you don't feel that you're enough for them. If your partner is emotionally mature and intelligent, they will understand you, support you and tell you that you have nothing to be afraid of. If you communicate your message in a constructive manner, it can build bridges between you. If you accuse them unrightfully, bridges will burn.

Well-packaged jealousy and whatever the trigger may be can be constructive in improving the relationship, or ending it. Unleashed jealousy will never bring anything constructive or good.

Another piece of advice: beware your friends in this matter. It actually depends on how you present your story to your friends. If you are impartial and tell the plain facts objectively, your friends may get a less biased picture and can give you more accurate advice. The thing with jealousy is that it's a very powerful negative emotion, and it's so tempting to passionately pour it out to someone who understands and agrees with you. Creating negative echoes around you won't help you see the clear picture. You'll just get more and more caught up in your imaginary and unproven accusations.

My advice here would be to keep your jealous thoughts to yourself unless you can talk about them objectively. Even then, your friends are your friends, so they should be on your side. It is good to feel supported, but if you want to find the truth about your jealousy, or want to find a solution for your envy, then try to deal with it by yourself, or enlist an impartial source as a specialist.

"I talked about my jealousy issues with my best friend. He had the best intentions when he tried to give me advice, but I didn't consider that he had bad experiences in the exact same situation as I did. He told me that my girlfriend was unfaithful for sure. I took his advice, and at home I lashed out on her. However, it turned out that the guy I saw her with was her cousin who just came back from a long trip. I felt really ashamed of myself, I apologized, but the damage was already done. We're still together, but there has been a weird atmosphere between us since then. I'm not angry with my friend. I know that he just wanted to help, but I should have known that he couldn't be impartial in this matter." (José, 24, Mexico City)

Jealousy is not love, one has nothing to do with the other. Don't mistake feeling jealousy as an act of love. It's an act of insecurity and a lack of control.

If your partner acts jealous with you, draw your boundaries. Do not let yourself get bullied and questioned if you find it unfair. Gently but firmly tell them, "If you use this tone and throw things around, I will leave and sleep at my parents' house tonight," or "I will answer all your questions, but only once. Please don't ask them again, the answer will be no different," or, "I understand how you feel, but I won't isolate myself from my friends."

Keep yourself to your words. Do not isolate yourself from the people you like. Rather, seek another solution. In the friend's case, for example, introduce your partner to them, take your partner out with you a few times so they get to know the subject of their jealousy. In most cases, they'll cool off when they see there's nothing to be jealous about.

My current partner has mostly female friends. I felt weird about it at the beginning, but now one of them is my best friend, and all the others are good acquaintances, too.

Stop constantly suspect and hating your gender's members. Not all women are easy, and not all men are conquistadors. I feel that especially among women there is a deep resentment when it comes to relationships. Sometimes it can escalate to a crazy level. Why couldn't your partner have female friends? Someone who wants to cheat will cheat. The subject of cheating usually is not in your inner circle or titled as a friend, anyway.

Another tip I give to my friends is about their current partner's exes. The ex-girlfriend or boyfriend represents the least threat to them. Why? They are the "tried and not compatible" elements. They are the ones your partner didn't want for a reason. That relationship ended for some reason and the odds are very small that they will get back together.

Jealousy is a waste of time, energy and emotions. Be mindful about it, and strengthen the bond between you and your partner by being honest and rational about it.

Chapter 13: How to Handle Cheating

February 5th, 2009

"I'm sitting on a bus, going home from work. I've lived in the capital for one month now. The most difficult month ever. Briefly, two moths ago we both got answers from the places where we applied for a job. I got the job, Dimitri didn't. After endless begging and fights, we agreed that I take this job, settle in the capital and he would follow me as soon as he got a reply from somewhere else.

Now I live with roommates again in a very nice neighborhood and make almost four times the money I did before. In the first two weeks, Dimitri was very compassionate and kind with me. I missed him badly and he said he did too. Two weeks ago he suddenly started a fight with me about how we should get over the temporary separation and stop nagging him about it. It was like a shock. Now, each Wednesday and on the weekend I travel back to him. He moved back home. Wednesdays I finish work at 1:30 p.m. so I can catch the fast train to go to him. The trip takes three hours, but I don't mind. The nasty parts are Monday and Thursday mornings when I have to get up at 4 a.m. to get into the office at 8. He can't come, he doesn't have the money.

He also started attending some weekend school to be busier. The school is in a different town than where he lives, so we technically only meet on Wednesday, Friday, Saturday and Sunday evening for a few hours. We fight a lot and I get desperate. Yesterday he became so angry about something that he took the knife out again. He "killed" the other door of his wardrobe with it. It was frightening, but I'm not so shocked anymore."

July 10th, 2009

"Dimitri has a summer camp for a month with his weekend school. It's some sort of field work. He is very happy about it, but he'll move to the other side of the country for this one month. I'm not happy about that. We spent a week together, and I just got back to work. It was chaotic. In the past few months he started telling me that he feels he'll die in the next eight years. I don't know why he says this, but it makes me very anxious, just as much as I hate when he talks badly about himself. I feel like he knows what to say and how to say it to corner me, and I'm so afraid that he'll leave me that I always enter into his game, even if I feel on a gut level that it's not okay. Sometimes I think how my life would be without him, but then I feel deeply guilty. He loves me so much and I act like an idiot. I should worship his patience with me more. Nobody ever loved me or ever will love me as much as he does"

July 30th, 2009

"Today Dimitri visited me for a day. It was so good seeing him! He told me he loves me and that I'm very important to him. That he'll move up to the capital when his school is over in autumn and we'll be together normally again. I feel that everything is falling back to the right place."

August 11th, 2009

"It's over. I just hung up on the phone with him. He called me to tell me that he is breaking up with me because he's in love with one of his colleagues at school. He asked me if I ever loved two people at the same time. He even told me that they kissed on the final evening, and he thinks it's correct to tell me it and break up with me. I feel nothing. I feel empty. I can't even say it hurts. It's a shock. I think I'll just go out to a bar and drink."

August 11th, 2009

"When I was at the bar my phone rang. It was Dimitri. He was very miserable. He cried and begged me to consider forgiving him because he loves me very much. To be honest, I am a bit upset. I know it's too early to claim such things, but I felt relieved that he just exited my life with a good enough reason for me not be so sorry about the breakup. And now, he planted a bug in my ear that we still have a chance together. Of course, I couldn't say no. I told him that he must arrive by tomorrow when I finish work. It will be Wednesday, so I finish early at 1:30 pm. I call my friend from work, I really need a friend right now."

August 12th, 2009

"Dimitri was uncommonly punctual. He waited in front of my office with flowers. He cried and was uncommonly silent. I was too. I didn't know what to say, but on a gut level I felt that he wasn't completely honest with me. We had talked for almost four hours when he confessed that he not only kissed that girl but also slept with her. I knew it, somewhere deep I knew it, but I hoped it wasn't true. He told me that the girl waited naked in his room for him, as though she was so strong that she could force herself onto him if he didn't want it. It was a mess. I feel something break inside of me. All my dreams of being together with him, growing old together, buying a little house with a garden where I could have cats and flowers seemed as the distant, childish

159

wishes of an inexperienced soul. I felt disappointed. I know that this relationship is far from being perfect, I'm far from being perfect, but I felt that I didn't deserve this. I felt dirty, I felt he was dirty, everything about it was dirty.

"My dad and his girlfriend warned me many times that I shouldn't be so addicted and devoted to this relationship, that I should take care. It's my first serious one, but it might not be the last. I hated them for saying these things. Lately I haven't even spoken with my parents and friends who talked against him. Maybe I was wrong. I need people who truly love me so much now. Anybody but Dimitri. But I can't have them. I live far away, I'm alone. I knew that if I don't forgive him in that very moment I never will, and I might never see him again. The thought of that being the last time I see him, I hear his voice, see his smile was even more painful than the cheating. So, I chose to give him a last chance."

Elena's notes:

Being jealous and having a clear proof of being

cheated on are two totally different things. Jealousy is an emotion that is triggered by assumptions, and the negative feelings you feel when cheated are based on fact. Therefore, they have to be addressed differently.

When it comes to handling a cheating partner, the first and most important thing you have to decide is whether or not you *can* and *want* to forgive them.

If not, then you should end the relationship quickly and start recovering from both wounds. The worst you can do is stick to the relationship for the reason of seeking revenge, or out of fear of change. It will poison your soul. Even if you seek revenge, you can't do it without hurting yourself. Have faith in fate. Honestly.

Let me tell you what happened with Dimitri a few years after we broke up, because we did. He became a couple with this colleague of his, the girl with whom he cheated on me. They both got fired from their workplace. Dimitri's parents hated the girl, she didn't even go to them. In the end, the girl left him when he got became ill and was hospitalized. However, Dimitri didn't get too lonely. By that time, he had another parallel relationship with someone else. He was a serial philanderer. I'd say, karma knows.

Let's get back to handling a cheating partner. You must be very honest with yourself – if only once in your life, this is the moment. If you truly feel that your partner can be forgiven because you consider the circumstances justifiable, or you feel that you had a major role in making this event happen, then take the time to accept this decision. Sleep a few times on it. If, after a few days, you're still sure that you want to forgive them, communicate it with your partner.

There are some things you may want to consider before making a decision. Is your partner truly sorry for hurting you? Did they confess the mistake they made voluntarily, or did you find out from someone else? Is this the first time he or she cheated? Do they treat you generally well or disrespectfully? Is your partner ready to make major changes to help you both ease your minds and move on? (For example, if they cheated on you with a colleague, do they offer to change jobs and/or move, etc.?) And, most importantly, can you trust your partner again? Can you believe that they won't do it again? If your answer to any of these questions is "no," then the relationship is pretty much done.

Take your time with the decision. Don't make the same mistake I did. I harshly rushed into a decision because, and this is the fun part, I knew if I didn't forgive him on the spot, I never would. It doesn't even make sense. Also, before you decide whether or not you want to forgive your partner, try to understand the motives why they cheated.

Tell your partner, "I really need to know why you do it. I need to understand your motives, otherwise I can't make a decision of what to do with us." Cheating isn't always about sex. People may cheat when they need an emotional connection, feel misunderstood, or go through a critical time.

Sometimes even your partner doesn't know why he or she cheats. Certainly, there is a reason, but it may not be conscious since he or she never thought about it consciously. So, if you get "I don't know" for an answer, it might be the honest one.

Reasons for cheating may vary from attraction to another person, to desire for attention, or novelty through poor communication, stress in the relationship, growing apart, cultural tolerance for infidelity, unfaithful parents, to even mental illness. Problems such as depression, attention deficit, or bipolar disorder, can all be the reason for poor decision making.

If you are ready to accept your partners' reasons for cheating for the moment, make the next step: ask them to cut all connections with the person (or people) they cheated with. It is impossible to move on if they still keep in touch with the third party. If for some reason your partner refuses to cut all contact, it might mean that he or she is not really willing to stop cheating. I would not recommend trying to fix anything if the partner is hesitant in breaking contact.

If the third party harasses your partner, even

when it was made clear that the affair is over, you can reach out to the authorities for a restraining order. It is not crazy, but entirely justifiable. Your peace of mind needs to be placed above everything else.

When you are ready, talk to your partner. Until then, you have every right to refuse to talk. "Sorry, but I still feel too hurt right now to talk." You're entitled to be very, very angry. Don't suppress your feelings of hurt, anger, and fury. It has to come out. Expressing it is healthy, keeping it in is toxic. To be cheated on is not a small thing, and your partner needs to know how their actions affected you. If you're not honest about it at the beginning, it will backfire later and make more damage and confusion. You have to express your anger when you feel it. It's not something you can "handle" later.

If you decide to forgive your partner, commit that you'll try to do it to your best knowledge and ability. Don't torment your partner day and night about the cheating. Not only for your partner's sake, but your own, as well. Rather, agree upon an hour one day when you talk about it, and try to avoid the topic the rest of the week.

It doesn't help the healing process to keep the shadow of the past alive with every breath you take. And, as mentioned before, don't forgive only to cripple your partner emotionally. Their actions were not correct, but if you stay only to make their life miserable, you won't be correct either.

Specify to your partner what details of the affair you absolutely don't want to know, and which parts where you expect honesty.

Build a stronger relationship, and take care of each other's needs. This is not a short, easy, and sacrifice-free process. You have to be very clear about your boundaries and what you need to be able to reestablish the lost trust. You can sound harsh sometimes. You can ask your partner to avoid going out for drinks with a single colleague of the opposite sex, even if the colleague is married. You can also ask your partner to report his or her whereabouts more frequently, especially at questionable hours. These might seem too much, but regaining trust because of cheating is extremely hard.

Let your partner know that your willingness to forgive doesn't mean that it will happen overnight. A few kind words and apologizes don't have to satisfy your need for seeking regret. You can say, "I appreciate your apologies, and I want you to keep on with them. But, for now I'm still not there to forgive you."

When you're ready, commit to repairing the relationship. This will require a lot of work and cooperation on both your parts. Be opened with each other, communicate often about your feelings, organize programs together, fall for each other again. Go on dates, do things you did at the beginning of your relationship. Learn about the other's love language and try to satisfy each other accordingly.

Know that this is not a blood contract. You can still end the relationship if you feel that even against your best intentions you can't move on from this disappointment. If you fight constantly, can't reconnect, don't show empathy towards one other, or you simply can't forgive him or her, it's time to move on. It's not your fault. Don't blame yourself for it, don't consider it as a failure. Very few people can overcome an affair. That's a very deep wound.

I can't forgive cheating, to be honest. I learned a lot in the past few years, became Zen and all, but I know enough about myself that if I get cheated again, I won't even try to forgive. I simply can't. It's not a lack of character, I don't torture myself for this. I'm just aware of myself. My partner knows my feelings and he's aware that cheating is a deal breaker for me. If you feel that you can't forgive cheating either, that's normal, too. Not everybody can. Accept and love yourself as you are, and be happy that you can admit this to yourself honestly.

One thing that can help relationships before cheating happens is to clearly communicate each others' boundaries. We're different. I know people to whom kissing doesn't count as cheating. I know others to whom much less is considered cheating. This is why it is crucial to tell your partner what your cheating boundary is early in the relationship so he or she doesn't overstep your tolerance line involuntarily. This discussion can save you from ridiculous excuses like "oh, I thought you're okay with it."

Chapter 13: The Point of No Return

December 24th, 2009

"I love my family. I'm so sorry I make them worry. I lost ten pounds in the last few months. I feel that I'm more miserable than ever. I try to get over the cheating but I can't. Dimitri now started working in the capital but we still don't live together. What's worse, that woman he cheated on me with lives in the same neighborhood as him and they are co-workers. He says I should trust him, but how could I? He said once he loved her. Now he says he doesn't. We fight each day, I feel like a psycho. I just look forward to New Year's Eve when I'll go to have a party with my old high school friends. Dimitri isn't happy about it."

January 3rd, 2010

"When I got back to the capital, Dimitri was waiting for me in front of my flat. He seemed so angry. Without even saying hi, he grabbed me so hard it hurt. He told me that he saw me sending songs to other men on Facebook. He hacked my Facebook and saw my messages with my old high school friend who was the DJ at the New Year's Eve party. I sent him some of my favorite songs to put on the playlist. I tried explaining it to Dimitri, but he didn't care. He told me I was cheating on him with that guy. Then he threw me against the wall, and it hurt pretty badly. He started smashing the garbage bins around us. I was so afraid that the neighbors would come out and hear it. I tried hushing him but he hit me in the face. Then, I think he just realized what he did. He told me again that he knows I'm lying and left. Now I try to ice my right cheek and reach him in between. Did he break up with me? I'm so afraid. I have to throw up again…"

January 6th, 2010

"Dimitri showed up today at my job. I haven't heard from him since that night. I lost four more pounds in the last three days. I have been throwing up every day, even though I haven't been eating. I was amazed at how much I could throw up. But my stomach was so restless. Yesterday my boss sent me home because I collapsed for no apparent reason in the middle of the office. She was very nice, told me to take a week off and get better, but I had to go in to work today. I go crazy just staying at home. So, he showed up. He kneeled in front of me in the middle of the street trying to apologize. He told me he drank and that some friend of his saw me dancing at the New Year's Eve party with a guy. That's why he was so upset. He begged and begged for forgiveness. I just nodded. He took me out to eat. After three days, it was the first time I actually could eat. He took me to the zoo and in the evening we went to see a football match. This day was better than it had ever been in the past year and a half. Maybe all these difficulties have strengthened our relationship and we'll come out victorious. I still believe we are meant for each other."

Elena's notes:

I have no excuses. I was weak and terribly

frightened. Every piece of my backbone and independence was removed by this point. This is the only explanation I can give retrospectively to my stubborn, irrational tolerance.

It was the only time Dimitri used physical violence to this extent. He didn't hit me too hard as far as I can remember, but the adrenaline was rushing so heavily in my body at that point I didn't even feel pain. Not physical pain, at least. I felt emptiness. Deep down at that moment was the confirmation that it was over. This was truly over. There was no way back from here, even if his actions later made me desperately try to overlook those events.

But, what is domestic violence? Justice.gov defines it "as a pattern of abusive behavior in any relationship that is used by one partner to gain or maintain power and control over another intimate partner. Domestic violence can be physical, sexual, emotional, economic, or psychological actions or threats of actions that influence another person. This includes any behaviors that intimidate, manipulate, humiliate, isolate, frighten, terrorize, coerce, threaten, blame, hurt, injure, or wound someone."

Now, reading this definition, I realized that I've been a victim of domestic violence long before it turned physical. I think a common mistake in everyday thinking is considering only physical aggression as domestic violence. Physical injuries (not fatal ones) heal much quicker than injuries of the soul. Still, people are only shocked when something physical happens.

Why? Maybe because physical violence can't be rationalized as much as feelings and emotions. If somebody hits you, that's a hit no matter how you may try to call it. If someone calls you mean names, you can explain it as the result of a bad day, wrong habits, and even make it out as something that didn't happen.

If you experience physical abuse, it's not normal, it's not healthy and you should not tolerate it. There is help out there. I collected some hotlines you can call if you're a victim of domestic violence, not only physical.

USA:

Office on Violence Against Women: Tel: +1 202-307-6026, Email: ovw.info@usdoj.gov

National Domestic Violence Hotline: Tel: + 1-800-799-7233, Email: hotline.requests@ndvh.org
Break The Cycle: This link shows each state's laws for violence http://www.breakthecycle.org/state-law-report-cards

If you're unsure who to contact you can always call 911.

UK:

24-hour National Domestic Violence
Freephone Helpline: Tel: +44 0808 2000 247, Urgency Tel. Nr.: 999

Europe:

This website collects more European countries' domestic violence contact: https://ec.europa.eu/anti-trafficking/citizens-corner-national-hotlines/national-hotlines_en. If you're unsure who to contact or your country is not listed above, call 112.

Australia:

Reach Out, Urgency Tel. number: 000. For more information visit this website: http://au.reachout.com/Emergency-Help

Canada:

This website collects the domestic violence hotlines of different Canadian regions, http://www.dawncanada.net/issues/issues/we-can-tell-and-we-will-tell-2/crisis-hotlines/. If you can't find your region or you face an emergency, call 911.

The rest of the world:

This website collects the emergency numbers of each country: https://travel.state.gov/content/dam/students-abroad/pdfs/911_ABROAD.pdf.

Know that abuse in any form is never justifiable. Your abusive partner will have excuses to justify the things that he or she does, but no matter what those excuses are, it is *not* a valid reason to abuse you. They will try to make it your fault. Don't believe it. It is not your fault. You were not asking for it whatever your partner says. Emotional or physical violence can never be a punishment. No one deserves to be abused.

Let's put aside the racial, religious, and gender-related BS. Everyone can be an abuser or a victim. And, not only female can be victims. This is another widespread stereotype when it comes to abuse. I encourage every man who experiences abuse he can't cope with to reach out for help! Even if the hotline he finds is for abused women, he can call them. Women can also access weapons, like knives and guns. They can be verbally and physically aggressive and abusive.

Don't stay oblivious to domestic violence. It can be dangerous even if your partner never lifts a finger on you. Some mental and emotional terrors can be much more harmful.

Make sure if you're indeed a victim. You can do this by knowing the law, consulting a specialist about it, and ultimately, if you feel cornered, humiliated, afraid, in terror or used. If you ascertain that you're a victim of abuse, take action.

This might not always be as easy as calling a hotline, especially if children are involved as well. If there is an emergency, of course, don't hesitate to call the hotline for immediate help. If there is no emergency, try to deal with the separation as smoothly as possible, if not for you, then for the sake of the kids.

Reach out to relatives, friends, a specialist and a lawyer. Prepare everything in advance. Contact only trusted friends who won't report your plans on leaving to your partner. However, make sure to involve a third party to have at least one person who knows about your situation.

You can set a code word for emergency cases, something neutral like "lemon soda." Establish that if you send only these two words to them, they immediately have to call 911 for you.

Talk to a lawyer about your situation, terms of

separation if you're married, and the kid's situation. I strongly suggest having a specialist with whom you can have honest conversations about your problems, who can give you mental support until everything gets sorted out during and after the separation.

Collect evidence about your partner's violent behavior, like pictures of the bruises, short notes with dates and locations pertaining to any abusive action you experience. Take care to hide them well enough so your partner cannot find them. I'd suggest electronic documentation in a coded or hidden folder. You can keep it in your Dropbox or ICloud. Transfer your evidence immediately after you make them, then delete them from your Folder and don't forget to empty the recycle bin, too. Have a picture of your passport, and your and your kids' important documents saved in your secret folder. You can never know if in the case of an emergency if you'll be able to collect them, even if you have them packed in an "escape bag".

Depending on your situation, the best thing you can do is have a bag prepared with some basic clothing, important documents and some money at the place of a trusted friend or family member, so that you can escape without worrying about things when an emergency situation occurs.

"I was terrified. It's the worst memory of my life. Tom came home drunk and started acting aggressively, forcing himself on me. He took and smashed my phone. My only saving grace was that I bought another phone, especially for an emergency event as this. I think it saved my life. I ran up to the attic where it was hidden and locked myself in there. I called the authorities and waited there until they came. Tom was charged with domestic violence and imprisoned for four years. I got divorced and moved. I hope he never finds me. I never want to see him again. Never." ("Phone2.0", 29)

A hidden backup phone can be a lifesaver as the above story proves. Always have your own bank account with a little money on it. Even if you have a "family account", never solely depend on that.

Important: Do not fight fire with fire. Don't become violent with your abuser. Don't try to solve the situation by yourself, always contact the authorities.

Chapter 14: Break Up Tactics

February 10th, 2010

"My birthday, and sort of our third anniversary. He took me out shopping and bought me Chanel lipstick. I never got such an expensive present from him before. The past month we've been very okay. We went out at least three times a week somewhere. I feel that everything is going well. He told me he loves me very much. He seems relaxed. I've gained three pounds so I don't like as a skeleton anymore. Oh, and I've got promoted. Now I'm the deputy manager of the sales section of the company I'm working at. My salary grew significantly and I have all of Wednesday free. What a happy change after so many atrocities. Finally, I can say I feel happy again."

"Yesterday he took me to his workplace. He showed me around. It was odd. Then, he started talking about our relationship being miserable, how unhappy he is and doesn't feel like we're heading anywhere. A month ago I could have agreed with it, but right now I feel these statements are a shock. I felt so confused. Suddenly a sense of terror ran through me. Is he breaking up with me? For real, this time? I tried to mumble reasons why we should still try, although I felt that these reasons were highly ridiculous, especially from my mouth. He was firm and distant. He pushed me away each time I wanted to get closer to him to embrace him or kiss him. I couldn't conceive how this distant, ice-cold person could be the same as the warm and affectionate one from my birthday. He told me he didn't want to ruin my birthday, and that day was like a goodbye for him. He took me to the metro station by car. I told him that if he wanted me to leave for real, then just spit it out. He said, 'Leave.' I felt like a higher power took charge over my actions. I felt like my soul was outside of my body. I saw myself opening the car door, step out and walk in the opposite direction like a machine. I heard him drive away with his regular aggressive engine racing. I didn't look back. I just walked and walked without direction. I stopped at a bus station and just stood there until it became dark, watching the buses pass. My brain was empty. My soul was annihilated. I was totally empty. But somewhere deep down I welcome this emptiness. I sensed it as a very painful, sudden, brutal emptying of my life to make space for something better.

"Today I spoke with my old Sensei, telling him what happened. As old habits die hard, I tried persuading him to speak to Dimitri, to change his mind and make him come back to me. He was responsible for our relationship in the first place. What he told me gave me the last kick I needed to completely, utterly, irreversibly bury everything I still felt for Dimitri. He said: 'I thought you guys hadn't been together for more than a month now. He's had a new girlfriend since New Year's." I hung up on him and dialed Dimitri. A woman answered. I need a drink."

Elena's notes:

Even if in those moments I felt very lost and alone, today I think our breakup was the best thing that could have happened to me, and for him, as well.

Break ups are never easy. I've pondered which is easier: to be the decision maker, or the party who is exposed to the other's decision? I've been on both sides and I really feel that being the one who makes the decision is much harder. My boyfriend after Dimitri was a really sweet guy. He was the total opposite of Dimitri actually, and this might have been the problem. He was the ultimate Yes Man – or should I say *Yes Ma'am*? I didn't have a clear reason to break up with him. I just didn't feel that our relationship was going anywhere.

Was it easy to make the decision? Yes. Was it easy to tell him? No. After a few weeks I knew this wouldn't work, but it took me almost a year to swallow my guilt, my fear of hurting him, and again, that annoying feeling that "nobody will love me as much as he does." Being on the other side made me understand why Dimitri could have been hesitant with our breakup, too.

Experiencing the other side always gives perspective. And, having this perspective, by experience I can tell that it's harder to be the executioner of the breakup.

Why? Because the decision weighs on your shoulders. What if you made a bad decision? What if you change your mind? What if you say the wrong thing? What ifs — a lot of them. The positive side of being the decision maker is that the event won't take you by surprise. You can be prepared to an extent.

If you're the one who has to face the decision, you may be shocked when you first hear it. Even if the breakup was expected, it's watching a horror movie the second time. You know the zombie will come, but you still get scared when it appears. However, after the break up happens and you settle for it, you'll have nothing else to worry about. It was not your decision, after all, and you can't help it. There is no relationship with only one person wanting it. If one party wants to leave it, that's the end.

I think that I just feared to become the decision

maker with Dimitri. I took the stupid attitude to wait until he did it. Of course, it was subconscious. My conscious mind kept trying to convince me that our zombie relationship is still alive.

Don't do this. Don't wait for the other one to say it. If you know that you want to end a relationship, if the thought of this option already nested itself in your head, that's pretty bad. Here, I'm not talking about situations when you guys have a fight and you're angry and hysterical and say things you don't mean (although it's better to talk about disputes in a calm way). I'm talking about casual, neutral afternoons when you start pondering how unhappy, bored, and dissatisfied you feel in your relationship, and have for a long time, and instead of thinking of fixing it, you'd prefer breaking up.

These decisions are never simple, especially if you are married, have children, common assets, you name it. As complicated your situation might seem, the decision is still very simple. Here is how I think break-ups and relationships should be weighed: it's your life versus everything else.

You have one life (at least right now), this moment is the first of the rest of your life. You're unhappy, and you probably don't have prospects to get happier with this person in the future (otherwise you wouldn't ponder on the break up).

What's more important? Your quality of life or anything else (family expectations, others' life, community opinions, and so on)? My answer is the former without hesitation. It's *your* life. I learned along my journey not to persuade people about my ideal life. It's not my right to do so. I just tell what I think, and it's up to you whether or not you agree. I wish you all the happiness you can get in this life, and save you from dying with regrets in a hundred years.

There are seven billion people on Earth. You can find a better partner among them even if it seems impossible now. That is something I can guarantee. I'm over two long-term relationships. I always thought that I'd never find someone better, and look at me now. I proved myself wrong each time. I feel that I got better as a partner, too. Each relationship taught me important life lessons without which I wouldn't be the person I am today. Therefore, I don't regret them. I just strive to not make the same mistakes again. That's what makes the difference. If you're better, your partner will be better too.

I feel I'm a bit ahead of myself because you're probably sitting with a huge Nutella jar in your lap, zillions of wet Kleenexes around you and you're watching The Notebook right now. You can't see the light at the end of the tunnel yet. Let me take you there.

First things first, don't try to be strong. Breaking up sucks. It hurts. It's painful. Your heart is torn apart. You feel lonely. You feel empty. Nothing seems right and there are no rainbows in the sky. That's normal. It would be weird if you didn't feel like this. Let the pain in. Take it, accept it, embrace it. Feel that you're human. Tears clean the soul, pain refines character. Don't fight against it. The quicker you accept what happened and cry it out, scream it out, pout about it, the quicker will it leave your system.

I chose to lock it in for two years. I pretended everything was okay, nothing hurt and that I was over it. Wrong. It doesn't work like that. Unaddressed and repressed negative emotions always backfire. In my case, I pushed my emotions so deep down that I became the notorious "man hater, emotionless, ruthless business woman of the company." In business life this attitude was helpful, but it was so unlike me. I felt burned out internally. I felt empty. Not break up empty –truly empty. *Life doesn't have a meaning* empty. Luckily, I realized this in time and I stopped the trend. I chose to leave my company at my peak to travel for an undefined period. *Eat, Pray, Love* with less pray and more eating, I guess. If I have any regrets with Dimitri, one would be not addressing my emotions of loss in time. I don't regret the three years spent with him, but I do regret the following two years living as a machine. I respectfully suggest you ditch the "tough nut" option for handling a breakup.

Surely you shouldn't mourn the breakup more than a few weeks, or even a few months either. No extreme is good. You'll feel it internally when your complaining is real, and when it turns into attention seeking. It's for your own good to mourn no more than necessary.

During a healthy mourning period you can be as self-centered as you need to be. Spend time with your friends, but find the right balance. If you spend each second of your life with someone just to avoid thinking about your ex, that won't help you. It will only extend the bitter time. Eventually, you'll be alone and repressed sadness can be much more intense if it is repressed for too long.

Have some alone time. You will have a lot on your mind after a breakup. It's likely that you need some time to think the events through. Even if you feel the need to be around people all the time because you're terrified of being alone, you should plan some dates with yourself, too. These are not regular dates. They are the sad, staring out the window, writing in your journal type of dates. Think about what happened, don't lock it away. Make some notes about your current feelings in your journal. It is amazing how visible the process of recovery is if you read the notes in six months. If you refuse to be alone after your break up, you won't be able to truly deal with it. Some feelings can be understood and handled at the time they are felt, now and later.

Pamper yourself. Allow yourself things you didn't before. Take a warm bath, go to see a game, whatever makes you feel better. As an extra tip I can tell you that when I started doing things Dimitri didn't like me doing I felt so much better. For example, he didn't like me eating unhealthy food, he didn't like me to wear red. I felt so good eating at McDonald's wearing a red dress. It seems like a childish move, but it is allowed in a post-breakup period.

Break all the connections with your ex for the time being. It is not impossible that you will end up being friends in the future, but I can guarantee you can't become friends instantly after the breakup. Let time heal your wounds first. If you were in a short relationship, you may be able to talk without any bitter feelings a few months later. If you were together for years, healing and overcoming the separation might take years as well.

Rely on your closest friends and family instead. If you're like me, you pretty much ignored all your other relationships while you were together with Mr. or Miss Ex. It's time to warm up old friendships, organize girl's or boy's nights, go out to dinner with friends. Go home, visit your parents, catch up with your siblings. Spend time with people who truly care about you. Pour out your soul to them, listen to their advice. However, don't talk to everybody about your sorrow because you may get stuck in a habit of complaining. Talk about it only with your most trusted circle.

Avoid social media. Don't look at what your ex is doing every five minutes. Also, resist the temptation to post photos about how wonderful you feel without him or her – even if you don't feel good. Log out of all your accounts and go have some real fun in real time and space instead. Facebook is not your friend during a breakup. If you know you won't be able to resist temptation, block your ex for a while. It is childish, again, I know, but it's an efficient method to not run into his or her updates all the time.

Know that nothing lasts forever: neither sadness nor happiness. It's not a consolation after a breakup, nevertheless, it's true. Even if the sadness doesn't last forever, it's normal to feel that it will for a short time. It's not unhealthy to hate life and pout over how unfortunate you are for a little while. All emotions should be accepted and released, as they are what you feel after a breakup. Most of these emotions are quite irrational, and even funny in retrospect, but when it's their time, they seem totally normal and justifiable. Don't be hard on yourself because of them. You can tell your friends that you want to be left alone one day, and call them crying the next, needing their support and company. You can feel relief over the breakup in the morning and be upset about it in the afternoon. Mood swings are normal in this period.

When you start feeling better, take the time to analyze your emotions related to the breakup. Let go of your bitterness and regret. These two are the most common emotions that you can feel after a breakup. These feelings are bidirectional. On one hand, you may be bitter because of what your ex did to you, on the other hand you might blame yourself for what you could have done differently. You can regret all the time you wasted on this dysfunctional relationship, or regret all those things that poisoned it. Bitterness and regret are a dangerous and slippery slope to self-hatred and feelings of inadequacy. The end of the relationship is not only your fault. It is always is because of both of you, even when it comes to breakups caused by cheating.

You're not a bad person. You're worthy of love, you are totally capable of having a good, healthy relationship – just not with your ex. That's all. Don't blame yourself more than necessary. If you regret saying or doing some things, make a note about them and strive to avoid them in the future. You can't rewrite the past, but you can shape your future better. That's where your focus should go.

Chapter 15: Epilogue

June 1st, 2012

"It's been two years and some months since I became single. I haven't written a journal entry ever since. I didn't see Dimitri, even though we live in the same city. Luckily it's big enough. I haven't dated anybody since then. I feel that I have strongly started compensating for all the injuries I've gotten in those three years. At the moment, I'm the manager of the company where I'm working, and the owner wants to make me CEO of his company when he retires in a few years. He has no kids and considers me an able leader. When he dies he wants me to inherit the entire company. It's a great privilege, although I worked for it. I took no holidays in the past few years, I worked on weekends, holidays – each day. I know everything about the company, I'm good at sales and marketing. Since I began working here, the annual revenue almost doubled. I feel that this is something I worked for and deserve. But I feel that I want to do something else. I may be totally crazy, but I think I'll turn down the offer. I need to find myself, to heal those wounds I just swept under the rug until now. I want to travel. I have enough savings. However, I'm bitterly aware that I might never be so lucky to inherit a stranger's company again."

June 4th, 2012

"I made my decision. I talked with my boss and turned down on his offer. However, I didn't expect his reply. He told me that he is happy to hear that I want to travel. He wants to be CEO for a few more years anyway, so I should take that time to go and travel. The only requirement he has is to help him with his work from a distance. The tasks require a few hours of work per week, and I can do them on my computer wherever I am in the world. Then, when I'm done traveling, he'll withdraw from the board. I said hell yeah! I'm so very happy! Now I start planning my few years of travel!"

July 4th, 2015

"Weirdly enough, it's Independence Day. I feel that I'm independent again. I'm healed. I just arrived at my last travel destination in Germany. My plane home leaves from Frankfurt in a few hours. It has been three long years and I saw much, experienced a lot. I've been in a long relationship, and I failed again – mostly because I was still not over Dimitri. But now, I'm ready to love again, grow again. I feel totally Dimitri-free. It took me five years.

"The past eight years have been a roller-coaster of emotions, experience, and endurance. Do I have any regrets? When I read some of my entries in the journal – yes, I do have many. Reading the journal as a whole, not many, except for those two years when I abandoned my emotions.

"Dimitri has been a very important milestone in my life. Many times I could have made decisions that would have made my life easier, but I didn't. I learned the hard way. Now I know and I'll be more vigilant in my next relationship.

"Now I sit in a café, and for a good twenty minutes I've been listening to a girl having a fight on her phone. A feeling just hit me... She's the one I should give my journal to. I wrote my journal with the purpose to give it to someone when I'm done, but I never actually believed I will. I feel that all the journaling, analyzing and self-healing has only served the purpose to pass it on to this girl! To you. I don't believe in coincidences, and I feel there is a reason why before writing these lines on my last travel day, before leaving home I hear you crying.

"I don't know you, I don't know your story. Maybe I'm wrong about you. Maybe your phone call is just a one-in-a-million occurrence, and otherwise you live in a happy relationship. If this is the case, then just ignore me. If, however, you feel unhappy, helpless and alone, just know that you're not. You're not alone in the world and you'll never be. My story might not be a happy one, but it certainly has a happy ending. I think reading through all my work in the past eight years you'll be able to connect, to feel understood, get comfort, or ultimately receive courage to change.

"You have one life to live, but not one love to give. People are only chapters in your book of life. As long as you draw breath, your book is not finished. It doesn't matter if a chapter has ended, your book is not finished! Never believe that you're not smart or worthy enough for better chapters! You are, and you'll have them.

"By the time you read these lines you probably have read the whole journal and formed your opinion. Maybe your decision, too. I chose to give this journal to you because I'm done. I'm healed and I feel that with its help you can heal, too. I hope you'll use it wisely, extract what is good for treating your wounds, and throw out all the rest. All relationships are unique, but good relationships are the same in one aspect: they grant you peace of mind, a mix of trust, security and mildly constant happiness. I believe in you!"

"Excuse me."

Someone was softly tapping my shoulder.
"We're closing in five minutes."

It was the barista. I got so carried away with Elena's journal that I didn't realize it had become dark outside. I still remember how the feelings of empowerment, sorrow, faith, awareness, amazement, self-respect, and survival instinct invaded my soul. I had so many emotions swimming inside me, I couldn't even describe them. My tears were flowing like a river. This journal was the sign, the confirmation I was expecting.

I got up, collected my things and went to rent a room in the first hostel I found in Frankfurt. I needed time to think, to finally think about myself. Not Norman's dog food and failed delivery. About myself and myself only.

I ended up spending five days in that Frankfurt hostel. I read Elena's journal again and again. During those five days I got to know all the faces of Norman — from angry and threatening, to begging and weeping. Each day he sent me different messages. I only replied to all of them with the same sentences: "I'm safe. I need to think. I may come back to you when I know what to say."

I knew I wasn't totally fair, but I didn't care. I needed time for myself, I put my needs first. And it felt empowering.

After those five days of contemplation, I decided to leave him and follow in Elena's footsteps and start traveling. I did it in a different style than she did, true. She had a successful career and made money doing it. I had nothing. What a change!

In 2006 I had everything, I was the daughter of a millionaire. She was living with others in a government sponsored, and probably trashy, room. By now she might have become a millionaire. I'm struggling to figure out what to do with my life. However, this is the wheel of fortune: sometimes up, other times down. I hit the low bottom and strongly believed that there was only upwards to go from there. I was right. I may not have the money yet, but I have my spirit, my freedom and peace of mind again!

Final Words

I'm in New York again. I just arrived a few days ago. I reconnected with my mother – she was so happy to see me. We couldn't stop crying for an hour. Appeasing my dad will be a tougher nut, but I'm sure he'll eventually come around and talk to me again.

I went back to doing what I can do best – write and telling stories. This is the first story I tell in a book form. The story of a chapter of my life, the story of a chapter of Elena's life.

The story of a chapter of your life.

I chose to write this book for the same reason Elena chose me to handle her precious journal. To help. I didn't have a serendipitous moment like she did when she chose me. My moment of serendipity was hers. I pledged to give back to the universe the good that she did with me. I hope this book will reach all of the people who need help to improve or get out of a bad relationship.

This book is like a pharmacy for sick loves. It has a pill for small illnesses and morphine for dying loves. It doesn't matter if you're lovesick or you live in a sick love – you'll find some help. If nothing else, a good laugh at how silly we human can be.

I wish you all the best on your journey. Know that you're not alone. I'm here in book form with Elena and many other people who experienced hardship in their relationship but overcame it. It's never too late and never in vain.

"Love isn't just a feeling, it's an art. And like any art, it takes not only inspiration. But also a lot of work."

Paolo Coelho

Made in the USA
Lexington, KY
06 April 2019